RI

GW00363077

Name ...

Address ....

....

....

I WAS CONFIRMED

in .... Church

on ....

I RECEIVED
FIRST HOLY COMMUNION

in .... Church

on ....

The Mass Book

With Selection
Of Prayers and Devotions

Contains:
The Order of the Mass
Morning, Night and Occasional Prayers
Prayers for Confession and Communion
Prayers, Novenas and Devotions

Imprimatur: Most Rev. J. McAreavey, D.D.
Bishop of Dromore
August, 2011

Reprinted 2018

C.B.C. Distributors
Website: www.cbcdistributors.co.uk

Contents

Patron Saints

Calendar of Saints

ORDER OF MASS
THE INTRODUCTORY RITES

Entrance Hymn or
Entrance Antiphon

C. In the name of the Father, and of the Son,
and of the Holy Spirit.
P. **Amen.**

GREETING
One of the following greetings is used:-

1. C. The grace of our Lord Jesus Christ,
and the love of God,
and the communion of the Holy Spirit
be with you all.
P. **And with your spirit.**

2. C. Grace to you and peace from God our Father
and the Lord Jesus Christ.
P. **And with your spirit.**

3. C. The Lord be with you.
P. **And with your spirit.**

PENITENTIAL ACT
*Then follows the Penitential Act to which the Priest
invites the faithful saying:*

Brethren (brothers and sisters), let us acknowledge our sins, and so prepare ourselves to celebrate the sacred mysteries.

A brief pause for silent reflection follows.

1. **All.** **I confess to almighty God
and to you, my brothers and sisters,
that I have greatly sinned,
in my thoughts and in my words,
in what I have done
and in what I have failed to do,**

And, striking their breast, they say:

**through my fault, through my fault,
through my most grievous fault;**

Then they continue:

**therefore I ask blessed Mary ever-Virgin,
all the Angels and Saints,
and you, my brothers and sisters,
to pray for me to the Lord our God.**

C.   May almighty God have mercy on us,
forgive us our sins,
and bring us to everlasting life.

P.   Amen.

Or:

2. C.   Have mercy on us, O Lord.
   P.   For we have sinned against you.
   C.   Show us, O Lord, your mercy.
   P.   And grant us your salvation.

C.   May almighty God have mercy on us,
    forgive us our sins,
    and bring us to everlasting life.

P.   **Amen.**

Or:

3.C.   You were sent to heal the contrite of heart:
    Lord, have mercy.   or: Kyrie, eleison.

P.   **Lord, have mercy.** or: **Kyrie, eleison.**

C.   You came to call sinners:
    Christ, have mercy.   or: Christe, eleison.

P.   **Christ, have mercy.**or: **Christe, eleison.**

C.   You are seated at the right hand of the Father
    to intercede for us:
    Lord, have mercy.   or: Kyrie, eleison.

P.   **Lord, have mercy.** or: **Kyrie, eleison.**

C.   May almighty God have mercy on us,
    forgive us our sins,
    and bring us to everlasting life.

P.   **Amen.**

*The Kyrie, eleison (Lord, have mercy) invocations follow, unless
they have just occurred in a formula of the Penitential Act.*

V.   **Lord, have mercy.**   R. Lord, have mercy.
V.   **Christ, have mercy.** R. Christ, have mercy.
V.   **Lord, have mercy.**   R. Lord, have mercy.

Or:

V.   **Kyrie, eleison.**   R. Kyrie, eleison.
V.   **Christie, eleison.**   R. Christie, eleison.
V.   **Kyrie, eleison.**   R. Kyrie, eleison.

GLORIA

This hymn is said or sung on Sundays outside
Advent and Lent and on Feasts.

Glory to God in the highest,
and on earth peace to people of good will.

We praise you,
we bless you,
we adore you,
we glorify you,
we give you thanks for your great glory,
Lord God, heavenly King,
O God, almighty Father.

Lord Jesus Christ, Only Begotten Son,
Lord God, Lamb of God, Son of the Father,
you take away the sins of the world,
have mercy on us;
you take away the sins of the world,
receive our prayer;
you are seated at the right hand of the Father,
have mercy on us.

For you alone are the Holy One,
you alone are the Lord,
you alone are the Most High,
Jesus Christ,
with the Holy Spirit,
in the glory of God the Father.
Amen.

THE COLLECT
P. Amen.

C. Let us pray
And all pray in silence with the Priest
for a while.

THE LITURGY OF THE WORD

Then the reader goes to the ambo and reads the
First Reading, while all sit and listen.
To indicate the end of the reading, the reader acclaims:

At end:
The word of the Lord.
P. Thanks be to God.

RESPONSORIAL PSALM

The people can respond at the beginning and after each
verse.

SECOND READING

At end:
The word of the Lord.
P. Thanks be to God.

ACCLAMATION

Said or sung by all. Can be omitted if not sung.

GOSPEL

C. The Lord be with you.

5

P. **And with your spirit.**
C. A reading from the holy Gospel according to N.
P. **Glory to you, O Lord.**

At end:
C. The Gospel of the Lord.
P. **Praise to you, Lord Jesus Christ.**

Then he kisses the book, saying quietly:
Through the words of the Gospel
may our sins be wiped away.

HOMILY

PROFESSION OF FAITH

I believe in one God,
the Father almighty,
maker of heaven and earth,
of all things visible and invisible.

I believe in one Lord Jesus Christ,
the Only Begotten Son of God,
born of the Father before all ages.
God from God, Light from Light,
true God from true God,
begotten, not made, consubstantial with the Father;
through him all things were made.
For us men and for our salvation
he came down from heaven,
At the words that follow, up to and including
and became man, *all bow.*
and by the Holy Spirit was incarnate of the Virgin Mary,
and became man.

For our sake he was crucified under Pontius Pilate,
he suffered death and was buried,
and rose again on the third day
in accordance with the Scriptures.
He ascended into heaven
and is seated at the right hand of the Father.
He will come again in glory
to judge the living and the dead
and his kingdom will have no end.

I believe in the Holy Spirit, the Lord, the giver of life,
who proceeds from the Father and the Son,
who with the Father and the Son is adored and glorified,
who has spoken through the prophets.
I believe in one, holy, catholic and apostolic Church.
I confess one Baptism for the forgiveness of sins
and I look forward to the resurrection of the dead
and the life of the world to come. Amen.

Instead of the Nicene Creed, especially during Lent and
Easter Time, the Apostles Creed, may be used - page 53.

*Then follows the Universal Prayer, that is the Prayer of the
Faithful or Bidding Prayers.*

THE LITURGY OF THE EUCHARIST

PREPARATION OF THE ALTAR AND THE GIFTS
*The gifts which will become the Lord's body and blood are
brought to the altar. During the procession of the gifts the people
may sing an offertory hymn.*
*The Priest, standing at the altar, takes the paten with the bread
and holds it slightly raised above the altar with both hands, saying
in a low voice:*

Blessed are you, Lord God of all creation,
for through your goodness we have received
the bread we offer you:
fruit of the earth and work of human hands,
it will become for us the bread of life.

P. Blessed be God for ever.

*The Deacon, or the Priest, pours wine and a little water
into the chalice, saying quietly:*

By the mystery of this water and wine
may we come to share in the divinity of Christ
who humbled himself to share in our humanity.

The Priest then raises the chalice above the altar and says:
Blessed are you, Lord God of all creation,
for through your goodness we have received
the wine we offer you:
fruit of the vine and work of human hands,
it will become our spiritual drink.

P. Blessed be God for ever.

Bowing, profoundly the Priest says quietly:
With humble spirit and contrite heart
may we be accepted by you, O Lord,
and may our sacrifice in your sight this day
be pleasing to you, Lord God.

Then the Priest washes his hands, saying quietly:

Wash me, O Lord, from my iniquity
and cleanse me from my sin.

C. Pray, brethren (brothers and sisters),
   that my sacrifice and yours
   may be acceptable to God,
   the almighty Father.

P. May the Lord accept the sacrifice at your hands
   for the praise and glory of his name,
   for our good
   and the good of all his holy Church.

Prayer over the Offerings
P. Amen

THE EUCHARISTIC PRAYER

Then the Priest begins the Eucharistic Prayer. Extending his hands, he says :

C. The Lord be with you.
P. And with your spirit.

C. Lift up your hearts.
P. We lift them up to the Lord.

C. Let us give thanks to the Lord our God.
P. It is right and just.

The Priest, with hands extended, continues the Preface. At the end of the Preface the people sing or say aloud:

All.
Holy, Holy, Holy Lord God of hosts.
Heaven and earth are full of your glory.
Hosanna in the highest.
Blessed is he who comes in the name of the Lord.
Hosanna in the highest.

In all Masses, the Priest celebrant is permitted to sing parts of the Eucharistic Prayer provided with musical notation, especially the principal parts.
In Eucharistic Prayer I, the Roman Canon, the words included in brackets may be omitted.

EUCHARISTIC PRAYER I

(THE ROMAN CANON)

To you, therefore, most merciful Father,
we make humble prayer and petition
through Jesus Christ, your Son, our Lord:
that you accept
and bless + these gifts, these offerings,
these holy and unblemished sacrifices,
which we offer you firstly
for your holy catholic Church.
Be pleased to grant her peace,
to guard, unite and govern her
throughout the whole world,
together with your servant N. our Pope

and N. our Bishop,
and all those who, holding to the truth,
hand on the catholic and apostolic faith.

Remember, Lord, your servants N. and N.
and all gathered here,
whose faith and devotion are known to you.
For them, we offer you this sacrifice of praise
or they offer it for themselves
and all who are dear to them:
for the redemption of their souls,
in hope of health and well-being,
and paying their homage to you,
the eternal God, living and true.

In communion with those whose memory we venerate,
especially the glorious ever-Virgin Mary,
Mother of our God and Lord, Jesus Christ,
† and blessed Joseph, her Spouse,
your blessed Apostles and Martyrs,
Peter and Paul, Andrew,
(James, John,
Thomas, James, Philip,
Bartholomew, Matthew,
Simon and Jude;
Linus, Cletus, Clement, Sixtus,
Cornelius, Cyprian,
Lawrence, Chrysogonus,
John and Paul,
Cosmas and Damian)

and all your Saints;
we ask that through their merits and prayers,
in all things we may be defended
by your protecting help.
(Through Christ our Lord. Amen.)

Therefore, Lord, we pray:
graciously accept this oblation of our service,
that of your whole family;
order our days in your peace,
and command that we be delivered from eternal damnation
and counted among the flock of those you have chosen.
(Through Christ our Lord. Amen.)

Be pleased, O God, we pray,
to bless, acknowledge,
and approve this offering in every respect;
make it spiritual and acceptable,
so that it may become for us
the Body and Blood of your most beloved Son,
our Lord Jesus Christ.

On the day before he was to suffer,
he took bread in his holy and venerable hands,
and with eyes raised to heaven
to you, O God, his almighty Father,
giving you thanks, he said the blessing,
broke the bread,
and gave it to his disciples, saying:

TAKE THIS, ALL OF YOU, AND EAT OF IT,
FOR THIS IS MY **B**ODY,
WHICH WILL BE GIVEN UP FOR YOU.

In a similar way, when supper was ended,
he took this precious chalice

in his holy and venerable hands,
and once more giving you thanks, he said the blessing
and gave the chalice to his disciples, saying:

TAKE THIS, ALL OF YOU, AND DRINK FROM IT,
FOR THIS IS THE CHALICE OF MY **B**LOOD,
THE **B**LOOD OF THE NEW AND ETERNAL COVENANT,
WHICH WILL BE POURED OUT FOR YOU AND FOR MANY
FOR THE FORGIVENESS OF SINS.

DO THIS IN MEMORY OF ME.

C. The mystery of faith.
P. We proclaim your Death, O Lord,
and profess your Resurrection
until you come again.

or:
P. When we eat this Bread and drink this Cup,
we proclaim your Death, O Lord,
until you come again.

or:
P. Save us, Saviour of the world, for by your Cross
and Resurrection,
you have set us free.

or:
P. My Lord and my God. *(In Ireland only)*

Therefore, O Lord,
as we celebrate the memorial of the blessed Passion,
the Resurrection from the dead,
and the glorious Ascension into heaven

of Christ, your Son, our Lord,
we, your servants and your holy people,
offer to your glorious majesty
from the gifts that you have given us,
this pure victim,
this holy victim,
this spotless victim,
the holy Bread of eternal life
and the Chalice of everlasting salvation.

Be pleased to look upon these offerings
with a serene and kindly countenance,
and to accept them,
as once you were pleased to accept
the gifts of your servant Abel the just,
the sacrifice of Abraham, our father in faith,
and the offering of your high priest Melchizedek,
a holy sacrifice, a spotless victim.

In humble prayer we ask you, almighty God:
command that these gifts be borne
by the hands of your holy Angel
to your altar on high
in the sight of your divine majesty,
so that all of us, who through this participation at the altar
receive the most holy Body and Blood of your Son,
may be filled with every grace and heavenly blessing.
(Through Christ our Lord. Amen.)

Remember also, Lord, your servants N. and N.,
who have gone before us with the sign of faith
and rest in the sleep of peace.

Grant them, O Lord, we pray,
and all who sleep in Christ,
a place of refreshment, light and peace.
(Through Christ our Lord. Amen.)

To us, also, your servants, who, though sinners,
hope in your abundant mercies,
graciously grant some share
and fellowship with your holy Apostles and Martyrs:
with John the Baptist, Stephen,
Matthias, Barnabas,
(Ignatius, Alexander,
Marcellinus, Peter,
Felicity, Perpetua,
Agatha, Lucy,
Agnes, Cecilia, Anastasia)
and all your Saints;
admit us, we beseech you,
into their company,
not weighing our merits,
but granting us your pardon,
through Christ our Lord.

Through whom
you continue to make all these good things, O Lord;
you sanctify them, fill them with life,
bless them, and bestow them upon us.

Through him, and with him, and in him,
O God, almighty Father,
in the unity of the Holy Spirit,
all glory and honour is yours,
for ever and ever.

The people acclaim:
Amen.

Then follows the Communion Rite page 30

EUCHARISTIC PRAYER II
PREFACE

C. It is truly right and just, our duty and our salvation,
always and everywhere to give you thanks, Father most holy,
through your beloved Son, Jesus Christ,
your Word through whom you made all things,
whom you sent as our Saviour and Redeemer,
incarnate by the Holy Spirit and born of the Virgin.

Fulfilling your will and gaining for you a holy people,
he stretched out his hands as he endured his Passion,
so as to break the bonds of death and manifest the resurrection.

And so, with the Angels and all the Saints
we declare your glory,
as with one voice we acclaim:

All.
Holy, Holy, Holy Lord God of hosts.
Heaven and earth are full of your glory.
Hosanna in the highest.
Blessed is he who comes in the name of the Lord.
Hosanna in the highest.

You are indeed Holy, O Lord,
the fount of all holiness.

Make holy, therefore, these gifts, we pray,
by sending down your Spirit upon them like the dewfall,
so that they may become for us
the Body and + Blood of our Lord Jesus Christ.

At the time he was betrayed
and entered willingly into his Passion,
he took bread and, giving thanks, broke it,
and gave it to his disciples, saying:

TAKE THIS, ALL OF YOU, AND EAT OF IT,
FOR THIS IS MY **B**ODY,
WHICH WILL BE GIVEN UP FOR YOU.

In a similar way, when supper was ended,
he took the chalice
and, once more giving thanks,
he gave it to his disciples, saying:

TAKE THIS, ALL OF YOU, AND DRINK FROM IT,
FOR THIS IS THE CHALICE OF MY **B**LOOD,
THE **B**LOOD OF THE NEW AND ETERNAL COVENANT,
WHICH WILL BE POURED OUT FOR YOU AND FOR MANY
FOR THE FORGIVENESS OF SINS.

DO THIS IN MEMORY OF ME.

C. The mystery of faith.
**P. We proclaim your Death, O Lord,
and profess your Resurrection
until you come again.**
or:
**P. When we eat this Bread and drink this Cup,
we proclaim your Death, O Lord,
until you come again.**

17

or:

P. **Save us, Saviour of the world,**
   for by your Cross and Resurrection
   you have set us free.

or:

P. **My Lord and my God.** *(In Ireland only)*

Therefore, as we celebrate
the memorial of his Death and Resurrection,
we offer you, Lord,
the Bread of life and the Chalice of salvation,
giving thanks that you have held us worthy
to be in your presence and minister to you.

Humbly we pray
that, partaking of the Body and Blood of Christ,
we may be gathered into one by the Holy Spirit.

Remember, Lord, your Church,
spread throughout the world,
and bring her to the fullness of charity,
together with N. our Pope and N. our Bishop,
and all the clergy.

....

In Masses for the Dead the following may be added.
Remember your servant N.,
whom you have called (today)
from this world to yourself.
Grant that he (she) who was united with your
  Son in a death like his,
may also be one with him in his Resurrection.

....

Remember also our brothers and sisters
who have fallen asleep in the hope of the resurrection,
and all who have died in your mercy:
welcome them into the light of your face.
Have mercy on us all, we pray,
that with the Blessed Virgin Mary, Mother of God,
with blessed Joseph, her Spouse,
with the blessed Apostles,
and all the Saints who have pleased you throughout the ages,
we may merit to be coheirs to eternal life,
and may praise and glorify you
through your Son, Jesus Christ.

Through him, and with him, and in him,
O God, almighty Father,
in the unity of the Holy Spirit,
all glory and honour is yours,
for ever and ever.

The people acclaim:
Amen.

Then follows the Communion Rite page 30

EUCHARISTIC PRAYER III

You are indeed Holy, O Lord,
and all you have created
rightly gives you praise,
for through your Son our Lord Jesus Christ,
by the power and working of the Holy Spirit,
you give life to all things and make them holy,
and you never cease to gather a people to yourself,
so that from the rising of the sun to its setting
a pure sacrifice may be offered to your name.

Therefore, O Lord, we humbly implore you:
by the same Spirit graciously make holy
these gifts we have brought to you for consecration,
that they may become the Body and + Blood
of your Son our Lord Jesus Christ,
at whose command we celebrate these mysteries.

For on the night he was betrayed
he himself took bread,
and, giving you thanks, he said the blessing,
broke the bread and gave it to his disciples, saying:

TAKE THIS, ALL OF YOU, AND EAT OF IT,
FOR THIS IS MY **B**ODY,
WHICH WILL BE GIVEN UP FOR YOU.

In a similar way, when supper was ended,
he took the chalice,
and giving you thanks, he said the blessing,
and gave the chalice to his disciples, saying:

TAKE THIS, ALL OF YOU, AND DRINK FROM IT,
FOR THIS IS THE CHALICE OF MY **B**LOOD,
THE **B**LOOD OF THE NEW AND ETERNAL COVENANT,
WHICH WILL BE POURED OUT FOR YOU AND FOR MANY
FOR THE FORGIVENESS OF SINS.

DO THIS IN MEMORY OF ME.

C. The mystery of faith.
**P. We proclaim your Death, O Lord,
and profess your Resurrection
until you come again.**

Or:

   P. **When we eat this Bread and drink this Cup,**
      we proclaim your Death, O Lord,
      until you come again.

Or:

   P. **Save us, Saviour of the world,**
      for by your Cross and Resurrection
      you have set us free.

Or:

   P. **My Lord and my God.** *(In Ireland only)*

Therefore, O Lord, as we celebrate the memorial
of the saving Passion of your Son,
his wondrous Resurrection
and Ascension into heaven,
and as we look forward to his second coming,
we offer you in thanksgiving
this holy and living sacrifice.

Look, we pray, upon the oblation of your Church
and, recognising the sacrificial Victim by whose death
you willed to reconcile us to yourself,
grant that we, who are nourished
by the Body and Blood of your Son
and filled with his Holy Spirit,
may become one body, one spirit in Christ.

May he make of us
an eternal offering to you,
so that we may obtain an inheritance with your elect,
especially with the most Blessed Virgin Mary,
Mother of God,
with blessed Joseph, her Spouse,
with your blessed Apostles and glorious Martyrs

(with Saint N. : *the Saint of the day or Patron Saint*)
and with all the Saints,
on whose constant intercession in your presence
we rely for unfailing help.

May this Sacrifice of our reconciliation,
we pray, O Lord,
advance the peace and salvation of all the world.
Be pleased to confirm in faith and charity
your pilgrim Church on earth,
with your servant N. our Pope and N. our Bishop,
the Order of Bishops, all the clergy,
and the entire people you have gained for your own.

Listen graciously to the prayers of this family,
whom you have summoned before you:
in your compassion, O merciful Father,
gather to yourself all your children
scattered throughout the world.

† To our departed brothers and sisters
and to all who were pleasing to you
at their passing from this life,
give kind admittance to your kingdom.
There we hope to enjoy for ever the fullness of your glory
through Christ our Lord,
through whom you bestow on the world all that is good. †

In Masses for the dead, the following may be said.

† Remember your servant N.
whom you have called (today)
from this world to yourself.
Grant that he (she) who was united with your Son in a
death like his,
may also be one with him in his Resurrection,
when from the earth
he will raise up in the flesh those who have died,
and transform our lowly body
after the pattern of his own glorious body.
To our departed brothers and sisters, too,
and to all who were pleasing to you
at their passing from this life,
give kind admittance to your kingdom.
There we hope to enjoy for ever the fullness of your glory,
when you will wipe away every tear from our eyes.
For seeing you, our God, as you are,
we shall be like you for all the ages
and praise you without end,
through Christ our Lord,
through whom you bestow on the world all that is good. †

Through him, and with him, and in him,
O God, almighty Father,
in the unity of the Holy Spirit,
all glory and honour is yours,
for ever and ever.
The people acclaim:

Amen.
Then follows the Communion Rite page 30

EUCHARISTIC PRAYER IV

It is not permitted to change the Preface of this
Eucharistic Prayer because of the structure of the Prayer
itself, which presents a summary of the history
of salvation.

C.   The Lord be with you.
P.   **And with your spirit.**

C.   Lift up your hearts.
P.   **We lift them up to the Lord.**

C.   Let us give thanks to the Lord our God.
P.   **It is right and just.**

It is truly right to give you thanks,
truly just to give you glory, Father most holy,
for you are the one God living and true,
existing before all ages and abiding for all eternity,
dwelling in unapproachable light;
yet you, who alone are good, the source of life,
have made all that is,
so that you might fill your creatures with blessings
and bring joy to many of them by the glory of your light.

And so, in your presence are countless hosts of Angels,
who serve you day and night
and, gazing upon the glory of your face,
glorify you without ceasing.

With them we, too, confess your name in exultation,
giving voice to every creature under heaven,
as we acclaim:

All:

Holy, Holy, Holy Lord God of hosts.
Heaven and earth are full of your glory.
Hosanna in the highest.
Blessed is he who comes in the name of the Lord.
Hosanna in the highest.

We give you praise, Father most holy,
for you are great
and you have fashioned all your works
in wisdom and in love.
You formed man in your own image
and entrusted the whole world to his care,
so that in serving you alone, the Creator,
he might have dominion over all creatures.
And when through disobedience he had
lost your friendship,
you did not abandon him to the domain of death.
For you came in mercy to the aid of all,
so that those who seek might find you.
Time and again you offered them covenants
and through the prophets
taught them to look forward to salvation.

And you so loved the world, Father most holy,
that in the fullness of time
you sent your Only Begotten Son to be our Saviour.
Made incarnate by the Holy Spirit
and born of the Virgin Mary,
he shared our human nature
in all things but sin.
To the poor he proclaimed the good news of salvation,

to prisoners, freedom,
and to the sorrowful of heart, joy.
To accomplish your plan,
he gave himself up to death,
and, rising from the dead,
he destroyed death and restored life.

And that we might live no longer for ourselves
but for him who died and rose again for us,
he sent the Holy Spirit from you, Father,
as the first fruits for those who believe,
so that, bringing to perfection his work in the world,
he might sanctify creation to the full.

Therefore, O Lord, we pray:
may this same Holy Spirit
graciously sanctify these offerings,
that they may become
the Body and + Blood of our Lord Jesus Christ
for the celebration of this great mystery,
which he himself left us
as an eternal covenant.

For when the hour had come
for him to be glorified by you, Father most holy,
having loved his own who were in the world,
he loved them to the end:
and while they were at supper,
he took bread, blessed and broke it,
and gave it to his disciples, saying:

TAKE THIS, ALL OF YOU, AND EAT OF IT,
FOR THIS IS MY BODY,
WHICH WILL BE GIVEN UP FOR YOU.

In a similar way,
taking the chalice filled with the fruit of the vine,
he gave thanks,
and gave the chalice to his disciples, saying:

TAKE THIS, ALL OF YOU, AND DRINK FROM IT,
FOR THIS IS THE CHALICE OF MY BLOOD,
THE BLOOD OF THE NEW AND ETERNAL COVENANT,
WHICH WILL BE POURED OUT FOR YOU AND FOR MANY
FOR THE FORGIVENESS OF SINS.

DO THIS IN MEMORY OF ME.

C. The mystery of faith.
P. **We proclaim your Death, O Lord,**
   and profess your Resurrection
   until you come again.

or:
P. **When we eat this Bread and drink this Cup,**
   we proclaim your Death, O Lord,
   until you come again.

or:
P. **Save us, Saviour of the world,**
   for by your Cross and Resurrection,
   you have set us free.

or:
P. **My Lord and my God.** *(In Ireland only)*

Therefore, O Lord,
as we now celebrate the memorial of our redemption,
we remember Christ's Death
and his descent to the realm of the dead,
we proclaim his Resurrection
and his Ascension to your right hand,
and, as we await his coming in glory,
we offer you his Body and Blood,
the sacrifice acceptable to you
which brings salvation to the whole world.

Look, O Lord, upon the Sacrifice
which you yourself have provided for your Church,
and grant in your loving kindness
to all who partake of this one Bread and one Chalice
that, gathered into one body by the Holy Spirit,
they may truly become a living sacrifice in Christ
to the praise of your glory.

Therefore, Lord, remember now
all for whom we offer this sacrifice:
especially your servant N. our Pope,
N. our Bishop, and the whole Order of Bishops,
all the clergy,
those who take part in this offering,
those gathered here before you,
your entire people,
and all who seek you with a sincere heart.

Remember also
those who have died in the peace of your Christ
and all the dead,
whose faith you alone have known.

To all of us, your children,
grant, O merciful Father,
that we may enter into a heavenly inheritance
with the Blessed Virgin Mary, Mother of God,
with blessed Joseph, her Spouse,
and with your Apostles and Saints in your kingdom.
There, with the whole of creation,
freed from the corruption of sin and death,
may we glorify you through Christ our Lord,
through whom you bestow on the world all that is good.

Through him, and with him, and in him,
O God, almighty Father,
in the unity of the Holy Spirit,
all glory and honour is yours,
for ever and ever.

The people acclaim:
Amen.

Then follows the Communion Rite page 30

THE COMMUNION RITE

(PRAYERS BEFORE AND AFTER COMMUNION PAGES 55 - 57)

After the chalice and paten have been set down, the Priest, with hands joined, says:

C. At the Saviour's command
and formed by divine teaching,
we dare to say:

**Our Father, who art in heaven,
hallowed be thy name;
thy kingdom come,
thy will be done
on earth as it is in heaven.
Give us this day our daily bread,
and forgive us our trespasses,
as we forgive those who trespass against us;
and lead us not into temptation,
but deliver us from evil.**

Deliver us, Lord, we pray, from every evil,
graciously grant peace in our days,
that, by the help of your mercy,
we may be always free from sin
and safe from all distress,
as we await the blessed hope
and the coming of our Saviour, Jesus Christ.

P. **For the kingdom,
the power and the glory are yours
now and for ever.**

Lord Jesus Christ,
who said to your Apostles:
Peace I leave you, my peace I give you,
look not on our sins,
but on the faith of your Church,
and graciously grant her peace and unity
in accordance with your will.
Who live and reign for ever and ever.

P. Amen.

C. The peace of the Lord be with you always.
P. And with your spirit.

Then, if appropriate, the Deacon, or the Priest, adds:
C. Let us offer each other the sign of peace.

Then he takes the host, breaks it over the paten, and
places a small piece in the chalice saying quietly:

May this mingling of the Body and Blood
of our Lord Jesus Christ
bring eternal life to us who receive it.

Meanwhile the following is sung or said:
Lamb of God, you take away the sins of the world,
 have mercy on us.
Lamb of God, you take away the sins of the world,
 have mercy on us.

**Lamb of God, you take away the sins of the world,
grant us peace.**

Then the Priest, with hands joined, says quietly:
Lord Jesus Christ, Son of the living God,
who, by the will of the Father
and the work of the Holy Spirit,
through your Death gave life to the world,
free me by this, your most holy Body and Blood,
from all my sins and from every evil;
keep me always faithful to your commandments,
and never let me be parted from you.

Or:
May the receiving of your Body and Blood,
Lord Jesus Christ,
not bring me to judgement and condemnation,
but through your loving mercy
be for me protection in mind and body
and a healing remedy.

*The Priest genuflects, takes the host and, holding it slightly
raised above the paten or above the chalice, while facing
the people, says aloud:*
Behold the Lamb of God,
behold him who takes away the sins of the world.
Blessed are those called to the supper of the Lamb.

All. **Lord, I am not worthy
that you should enter under my roof,
but only say the word
and my soul shall be healed.**

The Priest, facing the altar, says quietly:

May the Body of Christ
keep me safe for eternal life.

And he reverently consumes the Body of Christ.
Then he takes the chalice and says quietly:

May the Blood of Christ
keep me safe for eternal life.

And he reverently consumes the Blood of Christ.

> ### *Communion Hymn or*
> ### *Communion Antiphon*

When giving communion, the Priest says:
    The Body of Christ.

P.   Amen

While he carries out the purification, the Priest says quietly:
What has passed our lips as food, O Lord,
may we possess in purity of heart,
that what has been given to us in time
may be our healing for eternity.

PERIOD OF SILENCE OR SONG OF PRAISE

> C.   Let us pray.
>   *Prayer After Communion*
> **P.   Amen.**

THE CONCLUDING RITES

Any brief announcements are now made.

Then the dismissal takes place. The Priest, facing the people and extending his hands, says:

The Lord be with you.
P. And with your spirit.

The Priest blesses the people, saying:

May almighty God bless you,
the Father, and the Son, + and the Holy Spirit.
P. Amen.

On certain days or occasions, this formula of blessing is preceded, in accordance with the rubrics, by another more solemn formula of blessing or by a prayer over the people.

DISMISSAL:
The dismissal sends each member of the congregation to do good works, praising and blessing the Lord.
The celebrant says one of the following:

1. Go forth, the Mass is ended.
2. Go and announce the Gospel of the Lord.
3. Go in peace, glorifying the Lord by your life.
4. Go in peace.
P. Thanks be to God.

THE RITE OF
COMMUNION OF THE SICK

Greeting
The minister greets the sick person and the others present
in these or similar words:
The grace of our Lord Jesus Christ
and the love of God
and the communion of the Holy Spirit
be with you all.
All **And with your spirit.**

Sprinkling with Holy Water
A priest or Deacon may sprinkle the sick person and those
present with holy water with these or similar words:
Let this water call to mind our baptism into Christ,
who by his death and resurrection has redeemed us.
If the sacrament of penance is now celebrated, the
penitential act is omitted.

Penitential Act
The minister invites the sick person and those present to
recall their sins and to repent of them in these or similar
words:
My brothers and sisters,
to prepare ourselves for this celebration,
let us call to mind our sins.
The minister may continue with one of the penitential acts
from the Missal, or all may say: **I confess...**

The minister concludes:
May almighty God have mercy on us,

forgive us our sins,
and bring us to everlasting life. *All* **Amen.**

Liturgy of the Word
Several readings may follow, as at Mass. There should be
at least one reading, read by one of those present or by the
minister. A brief period of silence may follow the reading.
The minister may give a brief explanation of the reading.

Prayer of the Faithful
The prayer of the faithful may follow. The minister
introduces the prayer and says the concluding prayer. It is
desirable that someone other than the minister announce
the intentions.

LITURGY OF HOLY COMMUNION

The Lord's Prayer
The minister introduces the Lord's Prayer in these or
similar words:
Now let us pray together to the Father
in the words given us by our Lord Jesus Christ.

All say together:
Our Father...

Communion
Then the minister shows the eucharist, saying:
Behold the Lamb of God,
behold him who takes away the sins of the world.
Blessed are those called to the supper of the Lamb.

The sick person and other communicants reply:
Lord, I am not worthy
that you should enter under my roof,
but only say the word
and my soul shall be healed.

The minister goes to the sick person and, showing the sacrament says:
The body of Christ (or: The blood of Christ)

The sick person replies:
Amen.

Others present then receive communion in the usual manner.

Silent Prayer
A period of silence may be observed.

Prayer after Communion
The minister says the concluding prayer, for example:
Let us pray

Nourished by this sacred gift, O Lord,
we give you thanks and beseech your mercy,
that, by the pouring forth of your Spirit,
the grace of integrity may endure
in those you heavenly power has entered.
Through Christ our Lord.
All **Amen.**

Blessing

A priest or deacon gives the blessing in these or similar words:

May God the Father bless you.

All **Amen.**

Priest/Deacon May God the Son heal you.

All **Amen.**

Priest/Deacon May God the Holy Spirit enlighten you.

All **Amen.**

Priest/Deacon May almighty God bless you
the Father, and the Son, + and the Holy Spirit.

All **Amen.**

A minister who is not a priest or deacon, invokes God's blessing and makes the sign of the cross on himself or herself, saying:

May the Lord bless us,
protect us from all evil,
and bring us to everlasting life.

All **Amen.**

or

May the almighty and merciful God bless and protect us,
the Father, and the Son, and the Holy Spirit.

All **Amen.**

THE SACRAMENT OF CONFIRMATION
When the candidates have been presented, the bishop gives a homily or instruction about the Sacrament of Confirmation.

RENEWAL OF BAPTISMAL PROMISES

Candidates Stand

Bishop   Do you reject Satan and all his works and all his empty promises?

Candidates   **I do**

Bishop   Do you believe in God the Father almighty, creator of heaven and earth?

Candidates   **I do**

Bishop   Do you believe in Jesus Christ, his only Son, our Lord, who was born of the Virgin Mary, was crucified, died, and was buried, rose from the dead, and is now seated at the right hand of the Father?

Candidates   **I do**

Bishop   Do you believe in the Holy Spirit, the Lord, the giver of life, who came upon the apostles at Pentecost and today is given to you sacramentally in Confirmation?

Candidates **I do**

Bishop   Do you believe in the holy Catholic Church, the communion of saints, the forgiveness of sins, the resurrection of the body, and life everlasting?

Candidates **I do**

The bishop confirms their profession of faith by proclaiming the faith of the Church:

This is our faith. This is the faith of the Church.
We are proud to profess it in Christ Jesus Our Lord.

All   **Amen.**

THE LAYING ON OF HANDS

The concelebrating priests stand near the bishop.
He faces the people and with hands joined, sings or says :

> My dear friends:
> in baptism God our Father gave the
> new birth of eternal life
> to his chosen sons and daughters.
> Let us pray to our Father
> that he will pour out the Holy Spirit
> to strengthen his sons and daughters
> with his gifts
> and anoint them to be more like
> Christ the Son of God.

All pray in silence for a short time.
The bishop and the priests who will minister
the sacrament with him lay hands upon all
the candidates (by extending their hands
over them).
The bishop alone sings or says:

> All-powerful God, Father of our Lord
> Jesus Christ, by water and the Holy Spirit
> you freed your sons and daughters
> from sin and gave them new life.
> Send your Holy Spirit upon them
> to be their Helper and Guide.
> Give them the spirit of wisdom and
> understanding, the spirit of right
> judgement and courage, the spirit of
> knowledge and reverence. Fill them
> with the spirit of wonder and awe in

41

your presence. (We ask this) through
Christ our Lord.

All   **Amen.**

THE ANOINTING WITH CHRISM

The candidates stand before the bishop for the Anointing
with Holy Chrism. The sponsor places the right hand on the
candidate's right shoulder. The Bishop traces the sign of
the cross on the candidate's forehead.

Bishop   N., be sealed with the Gift of the Holy Spirit,

Candidate   **Amen.**

Bishop   Peace be with you.

Candidate   **And also with you.**

After Confirmation the Bishop talks to the candidates.
He may ask them to make a promise to refrain from all
strong drink until they are 18 years of age.

PRAYER OF THE FAITHFUL

Bishop   My dear friends:
let us be one in prayer to God our Father,
as we are one in the faith, hope, and
love his Spirit gives.

Priest   For these sons and daughters of God,
confirmed by the gift of the Spirit,
that they give witness to Christ
by lives built on faith and love:
let us pray to the Lord.

All   **Lord, hear our prayer.**

Priest   For their parents and godparents
who led them in faith,
that by word and example they may
always encourage them
to follow the way of Jesus Christ:
let us pray to the Lord.

All   **Lord, hear our prayer.**

Priest   For the holy Church of God,
in union with N. our Pope,
N. our bishop, and all the bishops,
that God, who gathers us together by
the Holy spirit,
may help us grow in unity of faith and love
until his son returns in glory:
Let us pray to the Lord.

All   **Lord, hear our prayer.**

Priest   For all men,
of every race and nation, that they
may acknowledge the one God as
Father, and in the bond of common
brotherhood seek his kingdom,
which is peace and joy in the Holy Spirit:
Let us pray to the Lord.

All   **Lord, hear our prayer.**

Bishop   God our Father,
you sent your Holy spirit upon the apostles,
and through them and their successors
you give the Spirit to your people.
May his work begun at Pentecost
continue to grow in the hearts of all
who believe.
(We ask this) through Christ our
Lord.

The Mass now continues in the usual way with the
preparation of the gifts.

Blessing
Instead of the usual blessing at the end of Mass, the
following blessing or prayer over the people is used.

Bishop   God our Father
made you his children by water and
the Holy Spirit:
may he bless you
and watch over you with his fatherly love.

All   **Amen.**

Bishop Jesus Christ the Son of God
promised that the Spirit of truth
would be with his Church for ever:
may he bless you and give you
courage in professing the true faith.

All **Amen.**

Bishop The Holy Spirit
came down upon the disciples
and set their hearts on fire with love:
may he bless you,
keep you one in faith and love
and bring you to the joy of God's kingdom.

All **Amen.**

Bishop May almighty God bless you,
the Father, and the Son, + and the Holy Spirit.

All **Amen.**

PRAYER OVER THE PEOPLE
Instead of the preceding blessing, the prayer over the people may be used.

Bishop	God our Father, complete the work you have begun and keep the gifts of your Holy Spirit active in the hearts of your people. Make them ready to live his gospel and eager to do his will. May they never be ashamed to proclaim to all the world Christ crucified living and reigning for ever and ever.
All	**Amen.**
Bishop	May almighty God bless you, the Father, and the Son, + and the Holy Spirit.
All	**Amen.**

"Prayer can truly change your life. For it turns your attention away from yourself and directs your mind and your heart towards the Lord. If we look only at ourselves, with our own limitations and sins, we quickly give way to sadness and discouragement. But if we keep our eyes fixed on the Lord, then our hearts are filled with hope, our minds are washed in the light of truth, and we come to know the fullness of the gospel with all its promise and life."

Blessed John Paul II

THE SIGN OF THE CROSS

*Christians begin their day, their prayers,
and their activities with the
Sign of the Cross.*

In the name of the Father, and of the Son,
and of the Holy Spirit.
Amen.

The Angelus

*For centuries the Church has recited this prayer
at noon and six in the evening in honour of the Incarnation*

The Angel of the Lord declared unto Mary; and she
conceived by the Holy Spirit, Hail Mary, etc. Behold the
handmaid of the Lord; be it done unto me according to Thy
word. Hail Mary, etc. And the Word was made flesh; and
dwelt amongst us. Hail Mary, etc. Pray for us, O holy
Mother of God, that we may be made worthy of the
promises of Christ.

Let Us Pray:

Pour forth, we beseech Thee, O Lord, Thy grace into our
hearts that we, to whom the Incarnation of Christ, Thy Son,
was made known by the message of an angel, may
by His Passion and Cross, be brought to the glory of His
Resurrection, through the same Christ our Lord. Amen.

May the divine assistance remain always with us. Amen.
And may the souls of the faithful departed through the
mercy of God, rest in peace. Amen.

Regina Caeli (Queen of Heaven)

*Traditionally recited in place of the Angelus,
during Eastertide*

V. Queen of Heaven, rejoice, alleluia.
R. For He whom you did merit to bear, alleluia.
V. Has risen, as he said, alleluia.
R. Pray for us to God, alleluia.
V. Rejoice and be glad, O Virgin Mary, alleluia.
R. For the Lord has truly risen, alleluia.

Let us pray. O God, who gave joy to the world through the resurrection of Thy son, our Lord Jesus Christ, grant we beseech Thee, that through the intercession of the Virgin Mary, His Mother, we may obtain the joys of everlasting life. Through the same Christ our Lord. Amen.

Glory Be To The Father

Glory be to the Father, and to the Son, and to the Holy Spirit; as it was in the beginning, is now, and ever shall be, world without end. Amen.

Grace Before Meals

Bless us, O Lord, and these Thy gifts, which from your bounty we are about to receive, through Christ our Lord. Amen.

Grace After Meals

We give You thanks, almighty God, for these and all your benefits, who live and reign, world without end. Amen.

Prayer to my Guardian Angel

Angel of God, my Guardian dear, to whom God's love commits me here. Ever this day (night) be at my side to light and guard. To rule and guide. Amen.

Hail Holy Queen

Hail, Holy Queen, Mother of Mercy; hail our life, our sweetness and our hope. To thee do we cry, poor banished children of Eve, to thee do we send up our sighs, mourning and weeping in this valley of tears. Turn then, most gracious advocate, thine eyes of mercy towards us; and after this, our exile show unto us the blessed fruit of thy womb, Jesus. O clement, O loving, O sweet Virgin Mary.

V.   Pray for us, O holy Mother of God.

R.   That we may be made worthy of the promises of Christ.

Mary is Mother of God and our mother. We can entrust all our cares and petitions to her. She prays for us as she prayed for herself: 'Let it be done to me according to your word.'

Hail Mary

Hail Mary, full of grace, the Lord is with you. Blessed are you among women and blessed is the fruit of your womb, Jesus. Holy Mary, Mother of God, pray for us sinners, now and at the hour of our death. Amen.

Memorare

Remember, O most gracious Virgin Mary, that never was it known, that anyone who fled to your protection, implored your help or sought your intercession was left unaided. Inspired with this confidence, I fly unto you, O Virgin of virgins, my mother. To you I come, before you I stand sinful and sorrowful. O Mother of the Word Incarnate, despise not my petitions, but in your mercy hear and answer me. Amen.

Morning Prayers

We thank you, Lord, for this new day which is now beginning. Help us to spend it doing what we can for you and for others, especially those who most need our help. I make this morning offering in union with the Divine intentions of Jesus Christ Who offers himself daily in the Holy Sacrifice of the Mass, and in union with Mary, His Virgin Mother and our Mother, who was always the faithful handmaid of the Lord.

Morning Prayer of Philaret of Moscow
Lord, grant me to greet the coming day in peace.
Help me in all things to rely on your holy will.
In every hour of the day reveal your will to me.

Teach me to treat all that comes to me throughout
the day with peace of soul, and with firm conviction
that your will governs everything.

In all my deeds and words guide my thoughts and
feelings. In unforeseen events let me not forget
that all are sent by you.

Teach me to act firmly and wisely, without
embittering and embarrassing others.
Give me the strength to bear the fatigue of
the coming day with all that it shall bring.

Direct my will. Teach me to pray. Pray yourself in me.
Amen.

Night Prayers
Dear God, thank you for your help
and guidance during this day.
Now I lay me down to sleep,
I pray the Lord my soul to keep
Angels watch me through the night
and wake me with the morning light.

Night Prayer - St. Augustine

Watch, dear Lord, with those who wake or watch or weep
tonight, and give your angels charge over those who sleep.
Tend the sick, Lord, and rest the weary. Soothe the
suffering and pity the afflicted: and all because
you love us, Lord. Amen

A Child's Prayer at Night

Matthew, Mark, Luke and John,
bless the bed that I lie on.
Before I lay me down to sleep
I give my soul to Christ to keep.

Four corners to my bed,
four angels there aspread,
two to foot and two to head
and four to carry me when I'm dead.

If I go by sea or land,
the Lord has made me by his right hand;
if any danger come to me,
sweet Jesus Christ, deliver me.
He is the branch and I'm the flower,
pray God send me a happy hour;
and if I die before I wake,
I pray Christ my soul will take.

Apostles Creed

I believe in God,
the Father almighty,
Creator of heaven and earth,
and in Jesus Christ, his only Son, our Lord,

At the words that follow up to and including
the Virgin Mary, all bow.

who was conceived by the Holy Spirit,
born of the Virgin Mary,
suffered under Pontius Pilate,
was crucified, died and was buried;
he descended into hell;
on the third day he rose again from the dead;
he ascended into heaven,
and is seated at the right hand of God the Father almighty;
from there he will come to judge the living and the dead.

I believe in the Holy Spirit,
the holy catholic church,
the communion of saints,
the forgiveness of sins,
the resurrection of the body,
and life everlasting. Amen.

Our Father

"The Lord's Prayer is the most perfect of prayers ... in it we ask, not only for all the things we rightly desire, but also in the sequence that they should be desired. This prayer not only teaches us to ask for things, but also in what order we should desire them."   St. Thomas Aquinas

Our Father who art in heaven, hallowed be Thy name; Thy kingdom come, Thy will be done on earth as it is in heaven. Give us this day our daily bread; and forgive us our trespasses as we forgive those who trespass against us. And lead us not into temptation; but deliver us from evil. Amen.

The Jesus Prayer

A very ancient, gentle and rhythmic prayer. It can be silently prayed meditatively on rosary beads, especially in the hours of stillness.

Lord Jesus Christ, Son of the living God have mercy on me, a sinner. *Repeat.*

Prayer Before Confession

Dear Jesus, help me to make a good Confession, Help me to find out my sins, help me to be sorry for them, help me to make up my mind not to sin again. Have mercy on me, O Lord, and forgive me. Mary, my mother, pray for me.

Confiteor

I confess to almighty God, and to you, my brothers and sisters, that I have greatly sinned, in my thoughts and in my words, in what I have done and in what I have failed to do, through my fault, through my fault, through my most grievous fault, therefore I ask blessed Mary ever Virgin, all

the Angels and Saints, and you, my brothers and sisters,
to pray for me to the Lord our God.

Act Of Contrition

O my God, I am very sorry for all my sins, because they
offend you who are so good, and with your help
I will not sin again.

Act of Sorrow

O my God, I thank you for loving me. I am sorry for all my
sins. For not loving others and not loving you.
Help me to live like Jesus and not sin again. Amen.

Prayer After Confession

Dear Jesus, thank you for helping me to make a
good Confession, and thank you for taking away
my sins. Help me, dear Jesus, never to offend you again.
Mary, my mother, pray to Jesus for me,
My dear Angel Guardian help me.

Prayers Before Communion

O my God, help me to make a good Communion. Mary,
my mother, pray to Jesus for me. All you holy Angels and
saints, pray for me. My dear Angel Guardian, lead me to
the altar of God.

Act of Faith:

O God, because you said it, I believe that I shall receive
the Body of Jesus to eat, and the Blood of Jesus to drink.
I believe this with all my heart.

Prayers After Communion

Jesus, I love and adore you,
You're a special friend to me,
Welcome, dear Jesus, O welcome,
Thank you for coming to me.
Thank you dear Jesus, O thank you,
for giving yourself to me,
Make me strong to show your love,
wherever I may be.
I'm ready now, dear Jesus,
to show how much I care,
I'm ready now to give your love,
at home and everywhere.
Be near me, Lord Jesus, I ask you to stay,
Close by me forever and love me I pray,
Bless all of us children in your loving care,
And bring us to heaven to live with you there.
Jesus you are with me now in all I say and do.

All I say and do today I say and do for you.
Jesus, stay with us but do not walk before us,
we may find it difficult to follow you.
Do not walk behind us, Lord,
we may find it hard to lead the way.
Just walk beside us, Lord, and be our friend this day.

Act of Faith:
O Jesus, I believe that you have come to me in
Holy Communion because you have said it and
your word is true.

Act of Love:
O Jesus, I love you. Make me love you even more.

Act of Thanks:
O Jesus, I thank you for coming to me in Holy Communion.

Prayer for Others:
O Jesus, bless my father, my mother, my brothers
and sisters and all others I ought to pray for.

Prayer for Help:
O Jesus, help me to do what you want me to do. Help me
to do my work better, help me to be kind and thoughtful at
home, and friendly to all my neighbours.

Prayer of Offering:
O Jesus, receive my poor offering. Jesus, you have given
yourself to me, now let me give myself to you: I give you
my body that it may be chaste and pure, I give you my
soul that it may be free from sin, I give you my heart that
it may always love you, I give you every breath that I shall
breathe and especially my last, I give you myself in life
and in death that I may be yours for ever and ever. Amen.

A Prayer For Those Who Live Alone
I live alone, dear Lord, stay by my side,
in all my daily needs be Thou my guide.
Grant me good health, for that indeed, I pray,
to carry on my work from day to day.
Keep pure my heart, my thought, my every deed,
let me be kind and unselfish in my neighbour's need.
Spare me from fire, from flood, malicious tongues,

from thieves, from fear, and evil ones.
If sickness or an accident befall,
then humbly, Lord I pray, hear Thou my call.
And when I'm feeling low, or in despair,
lift up my heart and help me in my prayer.
I live alone, dear Lord, yet have no fear,
because I feel Your presence ever near.
Amen.

Anima Christi
(The Soul of Christ)

Soul of Christ, be my sanctification;
Body of Christ, be my salvation;
Blood of Christ, fill all my veins;
Water of Christ's side, wash out my stains;
Passion of Christ, my comfort be;
O good Jesus, listen to me;
In thy wounds I fain would hide;
Ne'er to be parted from Thy side;
Guard me, should the foe assail me;
Call me when my life shall fail me;
Bid me come to Thee above,
With Thy saints to sing Thy love,
World without end. Amen.

Cross In My Pocket

I carry a cross in my pocket,
a simple reminder to me
of the fact that I am a Christian
no matter where I may be.

This little cross is not magic
nor is it a good luck charm.
It isn't meant to protect me
from every physical harm.

It's not for identification,
for all the world to see.
It's simply an understanding
between my Saviour and me.

When I put my hand in my pocket
to bring out a coin or key,
the cross is there to remind me
of the price He paid for me.

It reminds me too, to be thankful
for my blessings day by day,
and to strive to serve Him better
in all that I do and say.

It's also a daily reminder
of the peace and comfort I share
with all who know my Master
and give themselves to His care.

So, I carry a cross in my pocket,
reminding no one but me,
that Jesus Christ is Lord of my life,
if only I'll let Him be.

Prayer Of St. Francis

Lord, make me an instrument of your peace
Where there is hatred ... let me sow love.
Where there is injury ... pardon.
Where there is doubt ... faith.
Where there is despair... hope.
Where there is darkness... light.
Where there is sadness ... joy.
O Divine Master, grant that I may
not so much seek
To be consoled ... as to console,
To be understood ... as to understand,
To be loved ... as to love,
for .... It is in giving ... that we receive,
it is in pardoning ... that we are pardoned,
it is in dying ... that we are born to eternal life.

Prayer For Christian Unity

Look mercifully, Lord, on your people, and pour out on us
the gifts of your Holy Spirit. Grant that we may constantly
grow in love of the truth, and seek the perfect unity of
Christians in our prayers and our deeds.
Through Christ our Lord. Amen.

Prayer Before A Crucifix

Behold, O kind and most sweet Jesus, I cast myself on
my knees in your sight, and with the most fervent desire of
my soul, I pray and beseech you that you would impress
upon my heart lively sentiments of faith, hope, and charity,
with a true repentance for my sins, and a firm desire of
amendment, while with deep affection and grief of soul I
ponder within myself and mentally contemplate your five
most precious wounds; having before my eyes that which
David spoke in prophecy of you, O good Jesus:
'They pierced my hands and my feet; they have
numbered all my bones'.

Prayer For Employment

God, our Father, I turn to you seeking your divine help and guidance as I look for suitable employment. Give me the wisdom to guide my footsteps along the right path. I wish to use the gifts and talents you have given me. Please grant me this special favour I seek so that I may return to you with praise and thanksgiving for your assistance. Grant this through Christ our Lord. Amen.

Daily Prayer To St. Joseph
For Employment

Dear St. Joseph, You were yourself once faced with the responsibility of providing the necessities of life for Jesus and Mary. Look down with fatherly compassion upon me in my anxiety over my present inability to support my family. Please help me to find gainful employment very soon, so that this heavy burden of concern will be lifted from my heart, and that I am soon able to provide for those whom God has entrusted to my care. Help us to guard against bitterness and discouragement so that we may emerge from this trial spiritually enriched and with even greater blessings from God.

Followed by..... One Decade of the Rosary

Prayer For Exams

O God of wisdom, I thank you for the knowledge gained and the learning experiences during the year. Please guide me during my exams and help me so that I can perform to the best of my ability. Help me to remember what is truly important, as I focus my time and energy on these tests in the immediate future. Finally, may I sense your peace in knowing that I applied myself to the challenges of this day. I ask this through Jesus Christ our Lord. Amen.

Prayer For The Faithful Departed

November is the month when we pray for the faithful departed especially on November 2nd, the feast of All Souls.

Purgatory means that even after a person dies (provided he or she has not died in unrepented mortal sin), the mercy of God and the love and prayers of the communion of saints can embrace that person and help purify whatever might still need to be purified in order to see God "face to face". So it is very important that we always pray for the faithful departed, especially during the month of November.

Eternal rest grant unto them O Lord and let perpetual light shine upon them. May they rest in peace. Amen.

O God the creator and redeemer of all the faithful, grant to the souls of your servants departed the remission of all their sins, that they may obtain pardon, who live and reign for ever and ever. Amen.

May the divine assistance remain always with us and may the souls of the faithful departed, through the mercy of God, rest in peace. Amen.

TILL THE SHADES LENGTHEN
AND THE EVENING COMES
AND THE BUSY WORLD IS HUSHED
AND THE FEVER OF LIFE IS OVER
AND OUR WORK IS DONE
THEN IN HIS MERCY
MAY HE GIVE US A SAFE LODGING
AND A HOLY REST
AND PEACE AT THE LAST. AMEN.
CARDINAL NEWMAN

Prayer For The Bereaved

Almighty God, we rejoice to know that your reign extends
far beyond the limits of this life. In the mystery of what lies
beyond our sight, we pray that your love may complete its
work in those whose days on earth are done; and grant that
we who serve you now in this world may at last share with
them the glories of your heavenly kingdom; through the
love of Jesus Christ, our Lord. Amen.

Death hides - but it cannot divide
Thou art but on Christ's other side.
Thou with Christ and Christ with me
And so together, still are we.

it is written ...... Eye has not seen, nor ear heard, neither has it
entered into the heart of man, the things which God has prepared
for them that love him. Corinthians 2:9

Memories - God is always with us

THERE'S A PLEASURE IN THE KNOWING
AND A PLEASURE IN THE NEW,
THERE'S A SADNESS IN THE GOING
AND THIS I KNOW IS TRUE. THERE'S A JOURNEY IN A LIFETIME,
WHERE EACH MUST MAKE THEIR WAY, BUT REMEMBER AFTER
DARKNESS THERE COMES A BRAND NEW DAY. SO WHEN THE NIGHT
IS DARKEST, AND YOU FIND IT HARD TO BEAR, REMEMBER, WHEN
YOU'RE LONELY, THAT HE IS ALWAYS THERE.

Thanksgiving For The Life Of The Deceased

Blessed be the God and Father of our Lord Jesus Christ,
who has blessed us all with the gift of this earthly life
and has given to our brother/sister (Name)
his/her span of years and gifts of character.
God our Father, we thank you now for his/her life,
for every memory of love and joy every good deed
done by him/her and every sorrow shared with us.

63

A Prayer For Fathers

God bless all the fathers in this world. Guide them to be good role models and loving to all their children. Help them to be a father like You are. Give them grace and patience to handle situations in a loving way.

God our Father, in your wisdom and love you made all things. Bless men, that they may be strengthened as Christian fathers. Let the example of their faith and love shine forth. Grant that we, their sons and daughters, may honour and respect them always.

Prayer To The Holy Family

God our Heavenly Father, You call all people to be united as one family in worshipping You as the one and true God. You willed that Your Son become man, giving Him a virgin mother and a foster father to form the Holy Family of Nazareth.

We pray: may the Holy Family of Jesus, Mary and Joseph, image and model of every human family unit walk the spirit of Nazareth and grow in the understanding of its particular mission in society and the Church. May our families be living cells of love, faithfulness and unity, thus reflecting God's covenant with humanity and Christ's redeeming love for his Church.

Jesus, Mary and Joseph protect our families.

God made us a family.
We need one another.
We love one another.
We forgive one another.
We work together.
We play together.
We pray together.
Together we grow in Christ.
Together we love all people.
Together we serve our God.
Together we hope for Heaven.
These are our hopes and ideals.
Help us to attain them, O God,
through Christ our Lord,
by the power of the Holy Spirit.

Prayer For Grandparents

*This Universal Prayer for Grandparents was composed by
His Holiness Pope Benedict XVI in the Year 2008*

Lord Jesus,
you were born of the Virgin Mary,
the daughter of Saints Joachim and Anne.
Look with love on grandparents the world over.
Protect them. They are a source of enrichment
for families, for the Church and for all of society.
Support them. As they grow older,
may they continue to be for their families
strong pillars of Gospel faith,
guardians of noble domestic ideals,
living treasuries of sound religious traditions.
Make them teachers of wisdom and courage,
that they may pass on to future generations the fruits
of their mature human and spiritual experience.

Lord Jesus,
help families and society
to value the presence and roles of grandparents.
May they never be ignored or excluded,
but always encounter respect and love.
Help them to live serenely and to feel welcomed
in all the years of life which you give them.
Mary, Mother of all the living,
keep grandparents constantly in your care,
accompany them on their earthly pilgrimage,
and by your prayers, grant that all families
may one day be reunited in our heavenly homeland,
where you await all humanity for the great embrace
of life without end. Amen.

Prayer For Emigrants

O Jesus, who in the very first days of your earthly life were
compelled together with Mary, thy loving Mother, and Saint
Joseph, to leave Thy native land and to endure in Egypt
the misery and discomforts of poor emigrants, turn thine
eyes upon our brethren, who are far away from their
country and from all that is dear to them.
Be their guide in their uncertain journey,
their help in trouble, their comfort in sorrow;
keep them safe in their faith. Amen.

A Marriage Blessing Prayer

We thank you O God, for the love You have implanted
in our hearts. May it always inspire us to be kind in our
words, considerate of feeling, and concerned for each
other's needs and wishes. Help us to be
understanding and forgiving of human weaknesses
and failings. Increase our faith and trust in You and may

You guide our life and love. Bless our Marriage O God,
with peace and happiness and with your love.
Love is patient; love is kind. Love is not envious or boastful
or arrogant or rude. It does not insist on its own way; it is
not irritable or resentful; it does not rejoice in wrong doing,
but rejoices in truth. Love bears all things, believes all
things, hopes all things, endures all things. And now faith,
hope, and love abide, and the greatest of these is love.

Prayer For Mothers

I (we) thank you, creator of us all, for my (our) mother.
I thank you that she gave me life and nurtured me all those
years. She gave me my faith, helping me to know You and
to know Jesus and His ways. She taught me how to love
and how to make sacrifices for others.
Bless her with the graces she needs. Help her to feel
precious in your eyes today and to know that I love her.
Give her strength and courage, compassion and peace.
Bless her always with your love. Amen.

Prayer For Expectant Mothers

Almighty and everlasting God, through the operation of the
Holy Ghost, you prepared the body and soul of the
glorious Virgin Mary, Mother of God, to be a worthy
dwelling for your Son: through the same Holy Spirit you
sanctified St. John the Baptist before his birth. Deign to
hear the prayer of your humble servant. Through the
intercessions of St. Gerard, I implore You to protect me
(her) in motherhood and guard from the evil spirit the child
You have give me (her), that by your saving hand it may
receive holy baptism. Grant also that, having lived as good
Christians on earth, both mother and child may be united
in the everlasting happiness of heaven. Amen.

Motorist's Prayer

Grant me O Lord, a steady hand and watchful eye that no one shall be hurt as I pass by. You give life, I pray no act of mine may take away or mar that gift of thine. Teach me, to use my car for others need; nor miss through use of undue speed the beauty of the world; that thus I may with joy and courtesy go on my way.

St. Christopher, holy patron of travellers, protect me and lead me safely to my destiny.

Prayer For Others

Keep watch, dear Lord, with those who work, or watch, or weep this night, and may your angels care for those who sleep. Tend the sick, Lord Jesus, give rest to the weary, bless the dying, soothe the suffering, pity the afflicted, shield the joyous; and all for your love's sake.

SAINT AUGUSTINE

Let us Pray "Lord, help me live from day to day in such a self-forgetful way, that even when I kneel to pray my prayer will be for others".

Prayer For The Pope

Father, we pray for your protection and guidance over our Holy Father, the Pope. Give him strength and wisdom to stand as a prophet for our times. May he be a light in darkness around which we gather in hope. We ask you to bring about reconciliation through his faithful teaching of peace and justice. Grant him compassion and care to live the gospel in love and service to all people. Let him follow in the path of Peter and Paul, who, filled with the Holy Spirit, preached that the Lord saves all who call upon his name. Amen.

Prayer For Priests

Lord Jesus, you have chosen your priests from among us and sent them out to proclaim your word and to act in your name. Guide them and protect them in their ministry. Grant this through our Lord Jesus Christ, your Son, who lives and reigns with you and the Holy Spirit, one God, for ever and ever. Amen.

Serenity Prayer

God grant me the
SERENITY
to accept the things I cannot change.
COURAGE
to change the things I can and
WISDOM
to know the difference

Prayer For The Sick

Dear Jesus, Divine Physician and healer of the sick, we turn to you in this time of illness. O dearest comforter of the troubled, alleviate our worry and sorrow with your gentle love, and grant us grace and strength. We place our sick under your care and humbly ask that you restore your servant to health again. Grant us the grace to acknowledge your will and know that whatever you do, you do for the love of us. Amen.

Prayer During Visitation Of
The Blessed Sacrament

**ADORATION PRAYER
BY SAINT FAUSTINA**

I adore You, Lord and Creator, hidden in the Most Blessed Sacrament. I adore You for all the works of Your hands, that reveal to me so much wisdom, goodness and mercy, O Lord. You have spread so much beauty over the earth and it tells me about Your beauty, even though these beautiful things are but a faint reflection of You, incomprehensible Beauty. And although You have hidden Yourself and concealed Your beauty, my eye, enlightened by faith, reaches You and my soul recognises its Creator, its Highest Good, and my heart is completely immersed in prayer of adoration.

My Lord and Creator, Your goodness encourages me to converse with You. Your mercy abolishes the chasm which separates the Creator from the creature. To converse with You, O Lord, is the delight of my heart. In You I find everything that my heart could desire. Here, Your light illumines my mind, enabling it to know You more and more deeply. Here streams of graces flow down upon my heart. Here my soul draws eternal life. O my Lord and Creator, You alone, beyond all these gifts, give Your own self to me and unite Yourself intimately with Your miserable creature.

Prayer For Vocations
The harvest is rich, but the labourers are few
Lord Jesus Christ, Shepherd of souls,
who called the apostles to be fishers of men,
raise up new apostles in your holy church.
Grant them courage to follow you, who are the Way,
the Truth and the Life.
Bless those who are serving now with courage and
perseverance. Grant that many will be inspired by their
example and faith. We ask this through Christ Our Lord.
Amen.

Baptism in Emergencies Only
*Anyone, even a non Christian, can baptise in danger of
death, if they seek to provide as the Church intends.
Pouring, not sprinkling, water over the person say:*

I BAPTISE YOU IN THE NAME OF THE FATHER, AND OF THE SON, AND OF THE HOLY SPIRIT. AMEN.

*Contact a local Catholic priest after the baptism that the
baptism may be recorded in the local parish, even if
it took place in a hospital.*

The Beatitudes (GOSPEL OF ST. MATTHEW 5:3-10)

Blessed are the poor in spirit,
for theirs is the kingdom of heaven.

Blessed are they who mourn,
for they shall be comforted.

Blessed are the meek,
for they shall inherit the earth.

Blessed are they who hunger and thirst for
righteousness for they shall be satisfied.

Blessed are the merciful,
for they shall obtain mercy.

Blessed are the pure of heart,
for they shall see God.

Blessed are the peacemakers,
for they shall be called children of God.

Blessed are they who are persecuted for the sake of
righteousness, for theirs is the kingdom of heaven.

Act of Faith

My God, I believe in you and all that your Church teaches,
because you have said it, and your word is true.

Act of Hope

My God, I hope in you, for grace and for glory, because of
your promises, your mercy and your power.

Act of Charity

My God, because you are so good, I love you with all my heart, and for your sake, I love my neighbour as myself.

Seven Corporal Works of Mercy

Feed the Hungry
Give drink to the thirsty
Clothe the naked
Shelter the homeless
Comfort the imprisoned
Visit the sick
Bury the dead

Seven Spiritual Works of Mercy

Admonish sinners
Instruct the uninformed
Counsel the doubtful
Comfort the sorrowful
Be patient with those in error
Forgive offenses
Pray for the living and the dead

Seven Sacraments

Baptism
Confirmation
The Holy Eucharist
Penance
Anointing of the Sick
Holy Orders
Matrimony

Ten Commandments

1. I am the Lord your God: you shall not have strange gods before me.
2. You shall not take the name of the Lord your God in vain.
3. Remember to keep holy the Lord's day.
4. Honour your father and your mother.
5. You shall not kill.
6. You shall not commit adultery.
7. You shall not steal.
8. You shall not bear false witness against your neighbour.
9. You shall not covet your neighbour's wife.
10. You shall not covet your neighbour's goods.

Divine Mercy
Feast Day 1st Sunday After Easter
The Chaplet of the Divine Mercy

Opening Prayer: You expired, O Jesus, but the source of life gushed forth for souls and an ocean of mercy opened up for the world. O Fount of Life, unfathomable Divine Mercy, envelop the whole world and empty Yourself out upon us. O Blood and Water, which gushed forth from the Heart of Jesus as a fount of mercy for us, I trust in You. Amen.

(for recitation on ordinary rosary beads)

Our Father .... Hail Mary .... The Apostles' Creed.
Then on the Our Father Beads you will say the following words:

Eternal Father, I offer You the Body and Blood, Soul and Divinity of Your dearly beloved Son, Our Lord

Jesus Christ, in atonement for our sins and those of the whole world.

On the Hail Mary beads you will say the following words:
For the sake of His sorrowful Passion have mercy on us and on the whole world.

In conclusion Three Times you will recite these words:
Holy God, Holy Mighty One, Holy Immortal One, have mercy on us and on the whole world.

Closing Prayer: Eternal God in whom mercy is endless and the treasury of compassion inexhaustible, look kindly upon us and increase your mercy in us so that in difficult moments we might not despair, not become despondent, but with great confidence, submit ourselves to Your holy will, which is love and mercy itself.

PROMISES OF THE SACRED HEART OF JESUS

Of the many promises Our Lord Jesus Christ revealed to Saint Margaret Mary in favour of souls devoted to His Sacred Heart the principal ones are as follows.

1. I will give them all the graces necessary for their state of life.

2. I will give peace in their families.

3. I will console them in all their troubles.

4. I will be their refuge in life and especially in death.

5. I will abundantly bless all their undertakings.

6. Sinners shall find in my Heart the source and infinite ocean of mercy.

7. Tepid souls shall become fervent.

8. Fervent souls shall rise speedily to great perfection.

9. I will bless those places wherein the image of my Sacred Heart shall be exposed and venerated.

10. I will give to priests the power to touch the most hardened hearts.

11. Persons who propagate this devotion shall have their names eternally written in my heart.

12. In the excess of the mercy of my heart, I promise you that my all powerful love will grant to all those who will receive communion on the First Friday for nine consecutive months, the grace of final repentance: they will not die in my displeasure, nor without receiving the Sacraments; and my heart will be their secure refuge in that last hour.

SACRED HEART OF JESUS
Merciful Jesus, I consecrate myself
today and always to
Your Most Sacred Heart.

Most Sacred Heart of Jesus
I implore, that I may ever
love You more and more.

Most Sacred Heart of Jesus
I trust in You.
Most Sacred Heart of Jesus
have mercy on us.

Most Sacred Heart of Jesus
I believe in Your love for me.

Jesus, meek and humble of heart,
make my heart like Your heart.

THE HOLY SPIRIT
Come, O Spirit of Wisdom, and reveal to my soul the
mysteries of heavenly things, their exceeding greatness,
power and beauty. Teach me to love them above and
beyond all passing joys and satisfactions of the earth.
Help me to attain them and possess them for ever. Amen.

My hope is the Father,
my refuge is the Son,
my protection the Holy Spirit:
O Holy Trinity, glory to you.
All my hope I place in you, O Mother of God;
guide me under your protection.

INFANT CHILD OF PRAGUE

*Devotion to the Infant Jesus of Prague is devotion to
the Child Jesus. The image of the Child Jesus known as
the "Infant of Prague", was in reality of Spanish origin.
In the 17th century, this beautiful statue was brought to
Bohemia and presented to a Carmelite monastery. For
many years this statue has been enshrined on a side altar
in the Church of Our Lady of Victory in the city of Prague.
It is made of wax and is about nineteen inches high. It
is clothed in a royal mantle, and has a beautiful jewelled
crown on its head. Its right hand is raised in blessing; its
left hand holds a globe, signifying sovereignty.*

Divine Jesus, miraculous infant, kneeling before Your
sacred image, we implore You to hear our prayer. You
whose tender heart went out to all. You who gave sight to
the blind, healed lepers, made the deaf hear and the dumb
speak. You who brought the dead back to life grant us, we
beg You, the graces we humbly ask, through Your merits,
O Lord, Jesus Christ. Amen.

STATIONS OF THE CROSS

O God, you showed us in the passion of your Son the way to eternal glory by the Way of the Cross, grant that we may follow him now, by our prayers, to Calvary and may share his triumph with Him for all eternity. Amen.

1st Station: *Jesus is Condemned to Death*

We adore you O Christ and we praise you.

Because by your holy cross you have redeemed the world.

Dear Jesus you were condemned to death to free us from sin. May we be found worthy to be with you on the day of judgement and to hear you say "Come you blessed of my father".

2nd Station: *Jesus takes up His Cross*

We adore you O Christ and we praise you.

Because by your holy cross you have redeemed the world.

Dear Jesus, you said your burden was light, give us the grace to carry our cross gladly each day.

3rd Station: *Jesus falls the first time*

We adore you O Christ and we praise you.

Because by your holy cross you have redeemed the world.

Dear Jesus, you have seen me fall often and have always

helped me to rise again. Give me your grace that I may not fall again.

4th Station: *Jesus meets his afflicted Mother*

We adore you O Christ and we praise you.

Because by your holy cross you have redeemed the world.

Dear Jesus, you were comforted by your mother on your way to death. May we have her help now and at the hour of our death.

5th Station: *Simon of Cyrene helps Jesus carry the cross*

We adore you O Christ and we praise you.

Because by your holy cross you have redeemed the world.

Dear Jesus, you were helped by Simon. May we too help to lighten your cross by avoiding sin.

6th Station: *Veronica wipes the face of Jesus*

We adore you O Christ and we praise you.

Because by your holy cross you have redeemed the world.

Dear Jesus, you rewarded Veronica for her act of kindness. Help us to be kind to others that we may receive the reward of your friendship.

7th Station: *Jesus falls the second time*

We adore you O Christ and we praise you.

Because by your holy cross you have redeemed the world.

Dear Jesus, you came to save a fallen world. May we, by your example, help others who have fallen.

8th Station: *Jesus meets the women of Jerusalem*

We adore you O Christ and we praise you.

Because by your holy cross you have redeemed the world.

Dear Jesus, you consoled the women of Jerusalem who wept for you. Make us truly sorry for our sins so that we too may be consoled by you.

9th Station: *Jesus falls a third time*

We adore you O Christ and we praise you.

Because by your holy cross you have redeemed the world.

Dear Jesus, at the end of your journey you fall for the last time. May we come to the end of our journey without falling again into sin:

10th Station: *Jesus is stripped of his Garments*

We adore you O Christ and we praise you.

Because by your holy cross you have redeemed the world.

Dear Jesus, strip us of all feelings of pride. Give us the grace to be meek and humble like you.

11th Station: *Jesus is nailed to the Cross*

We adore you O Christ and we praise you.

Because by your holy cross you have redeemed the world.

Dear Jesus, you offered yourself willingly to the soldiers to be nailed to the cross. I wish to offer myself to you. Please help me.

12th Station: *Jesus dies on the Cross*

We adore you O Christ and we praise you.

Because by your holy cross you have redeemed the world.

O my God I am very sorry for all my sins, because they offend you who are so good, and with your help I will not sin again.

13th Station: *Jesus is placed in the arms of his Mother*

We adore you O Christ and we praise you.

Because by your holy cross you have redeemed the world.

Dear Jesus, your death brought sorrow to the heart of Mary your Mother. May we never add to that sorrow by our own sins.

14th Station: *Jesus is laid in the tomb*

We adore you O Christ and we praise you.

Because by your holy cross you have redeemed the world.

Dear Jesus, you arose after three days in the tomb. May we rise again on the last day to be happy with you for ever in heaven. Amen.

Prayer to Our Lady
The Immaculate Conception
Feast Day: December 8th

O Immaculate Virgin Mary, conceived without sin, remember, you were miraculously preserved from even the shadow of sin, because you were destined to become not only the Mother of God, but also the mother, the refuge, and the advocate of man; penetrated therefore, with the most lively confidence in your never failing intercession, we most humbly implore you to look with favour upon the intentions of this novena, and to obtain for us the graces and the favours we request. You know, O Mary, how often our hearts are the sanctuaries of God, who abhors iniquity. Obtain for us, then, that angelic purity which was your favourite virtue, that purity of heart which will attach us to God alone, and that purity of intention which will consecrate every thought, word, and action to His greater glory. Obtain also for us a constant spirit of prayer and self denial, that we may recover by penance that innocence which we have lost by sin, and at length attain safely to that blessed abode of the saints, where nothing defiled can enter.

O Mary, conceived without sin, pray for us who have recourse to thee.

Prayer to Our Lady of Fatima
Feast Day: 13th May
Let us pray
O God of infinite goodness and mercy, fill our hearts with
a great confidence in Your dear Mother, whom we invoke
under the title of Our Lady of the Rosary and Our Lady of
Fatima, and grant us by her powerful intercession all the
graces, spiritual and temporal, which we need.
Through Christ Our Lord. Amen.

Our Lady of Knock
Feast Day: 17th August
The Story of Knock
*At about 8 o'clock on the Thursday evening of 21st August
1879 the Blessed Virgin Mary, St. Joseph and St. John
the Evangelist appeared at the south gable of the church
at Knock, Co. Mayo, Ireland. Beside them and a little to
the right was an altar with a cross and the figure of a lamb
around which angels hovered. There were fifteen official
witnesses to the apparition, young and old who watched it
for two hours in pouring rain and recited the rosary. Two
Commissions of Enquiry accepted their testimony as
trustworthy and satisfactory in 1879 and 1936.*

*Today, Knock, ranks among the world's major Marian
Shrines, having enjoyed the full approval of the church for
many years. It has received privileges from four Popes
and the most recent privilege was the visit of His Holiness,
Pope John Paul II, on 30th September, 1979.*

Novena to Our Lady of Knock
In the name of the Father, and of the Son,
and of the Holy Spirit. Amen.

*Give praise to the Father Almighty,
to His son, Jesus Christ the Lord,
to the Spirit who lives in our hearts,
Both now and forever. Amen.*

Our Lady of Knock, Queen of Ireland, you gave hope to
your people in a time of distress, and comforted them in
sorrow. You have inspired countless pilgrims to pray with
confidence to your Divine Son, remembering His promise:-
'Ask and you shall receive, seek and you shall find'
Help me to remember that we are all pilgrims on the road
to heaven. Fill me with love and concern for my brothers
and sisters in Christ, especially those who live with me.
Comfort me when I am sick, lonely or depressed. Teach
me how to take part ever more reverently in the Holy
Mass. Give me a greater love of Jesus in the Blessed
Sacrament. Pray for me now and at the hour of my death.
Amen.

Prayer to Our Lady of Lourdes
Feast Day: February 11th
O God, who by the Immaculate Conception of the Virgin
did prepare a worthy dwelling for your Son, we humbly
request that we, who celebrate the apparition of the same
Blessed Virgin, may obtain health of soul and body through
the same Lord Jesus Christ, your Son, who lives and
reigns with you in the unity of the Holy Spirit, God, world
without end. Amen.

Our Lady of the Miraculous Medal

Feast Day: 27th November

The year of 1830 on the Miraculous Medal is the year the Blessed Mother gave the design of the Miraculous Medal to Saint Catherine Laboure.

FRONT OF MEDAL

Mary is standing upon a globe, crushing the head of a serpent beneath her foot. She stands upon the globe, as the Queen of Heaven and Earth. Her feet crush the serpent to proclaim Satan and all his followers are helpless before her.

BACK OF MEDAL

The two hearts represent the Love of Jesus and Mary for us. The twelve stars refer to the Apostles, who represent the Church as it surrounds Mary.

ACT OF CONSECRATION TO
OUR LADY OF THE MIRACULOUS MEDAL

O Virgin Mother of God, Mary Immaculate, we dedicate and consecrate ourselves to you under the title of Our Lady of the Miraculous Medal. May this medal be for each one of us a sure sign of your motherly affection for us and a constant reminder of our duties towards you. Ever while wearing it, may we be blessed by your loving protection and preserved in the grace of your Son. O most powerful Virgin, Mother of our Saviour, keep us close to you every moment of our lives. Obtain for us, your children, the grace of a happy death, so that, in union with you, we may enjoy the happiness of heaven forever. Amen.

*O Mary conceived without sin, pray for us
who have recourse to you.*
(Say three times)

86

Prayer To The Queen of the Rosary

O God, whose only-begotten Son by His life, death and resurrection has purchased for us the rewards of eternal salvation, grant, we beseech thee, that meditating on these mysteries in the most holy rosary of the Blessed Virgin Mary, we may imitate what they contain, and obtain what they promise. Through Our Lord Jesus Christ, who lives and reigns with God the Father in the unity of the Holy Spirit, God, world without end. Amen.

The rosary consists of 20 mysteries divided into four distinct parts - The Joyful, The Luminous, The Sorrowful and the Glorious Mysteries. Each mystery is represented by a decade made up of the Our Father, ten Hail Marys and a Glory Be.

THE ROSARY

The Joyful Mysteries
These are recited on Mondays & Saturdays

1st ~ The Annunciation
The Angel Gabriel tells Mary that she is to be the Mother of God

2nd ~ The Visitation
The Blessed Virgin pays a visit to her cousin Elizabeth

3rd ~ The Nativity
The Infant Jesus is born in a stable in Bethlehem

4th ~ The Presentation
The Blessed Virgin presents the Child Jesus

5th ~ The Finding in the Temple
Jesus is lost for three days and is found in the temple

The Mysteries of Light (Luminous Mysteries)
These are recited on Thursdays

1st ~ The Baptism of Jesus
Jesus is baptised in the river Jordan

2nd ~ The Wedding at Cana
Jesus attends a wedding at Cana in Galilee

3rd ~ The Proclamation of the Kingdom of God
*Jesus goes through the towns and cities proclaiming
God's Kingdom*

4th ~ The Transfiguration
*Jesus leads his apostles up a high mountain, where they see
him shining in glorious light*

5th ~ The Institution of Holy Eucharist
*At supper with his friends before He dies,
Jesus gives himself to them in bread and wine*

The Sorrowful Mysteries
These are recited on Tuesdays & Fridays

1st ~ The Agony in the Garden
Jesus prays in the Garden of Olives

2nd ~ The Scourging at the Pillar
Then Pilate took Jesus and had him scourged

3rd ~ The Crowning with Thorns
A Crown of Thorns is placed on the head of Jesus

4th ~ The Carrying of the Cross
Jesus is made to carry his cross to Calvary

5th ~ The Crucifixion
Jesus is nailed to the cross and dies for our sins

The Glorious Mysteries
These are recited on Wednesdays & Sundays

1st ~ The Resurrection
Jesus rises from the dead, three days after His death

2nd ~ The Ascension
Forty days after His death, Jesus ascends into heaven

3rd ~ The Descent of the Holy Spirit
Ten days after the Ascension, the Holy Spirit comes to the apostles and the Blessed Mother

4th ~ The Assumption
The Blessed Mother dies and is assumed into Heaven

5th ~ The Coronation
The Blessed Virgin is crowned Queen of Heaven and Earth by Jesus, her Son

After the Rosary

Hail Holy Queen (Salve Regina)

Hail, Holy Queen, Mother of Mercy; hail our life, our sweetness and our hope. To thee do we cry, poor banished children of Eve, to thee do we send up our sighs, mourning and weeping in this valley of tears. Turn then, most gracious advocate, thine eyes of mercy towards us; and after this, our exile show unto us the blessed fruit of thy womb, Jesus. O clement, O loving, O sweet Virgin Mary. Pray for us, O Holy Mother of God, that we may be made worthy of the promises of Christ.

V.   Pray for us, O holy Mother of God.
R.   That we may be made worthy of the promises of Christ.

Let us pray:

O God, whose only-begotten Son by his life, death and resurrection purchased for us the rewards of eternal life; grant, we beseech you, that meditating on these mysteries in the most Holy Rosary of the Blessed Virgin Mary, we may both imitate what they contain and obtain what they promise, through the same Christ our Lord. Amen.

PRAYERS AND DEVOTIONS

Prayer to St. Anne
Feast Day 26th July
MEMORARE TO ST. ANNE

Remember, good Saint Anne, whose name means grace
and mercy, that never was it known that anyone who fled
to your protection, implored your help or sought your
intercession, was left unaided. Inspired with this
confidence, I come before you, sinful and sorrowful. Holy
Mother of the Immaculate Virgin Mary and loving
grandmother of the Saviour do not reject my appeal, but
hear me and answer my prayer. Amen.

Prayer to St. Anthony
Feast Day 13th June
PRAYER FOR DIVINE PROTECTION

O dear St. Anthony, by your holy example and apostolic
life you led countless souls to the protection
of our Divine Lord. I beg of you, obtain that same
protection and guidance for me and those dear to me
during these times of dire distress. In your tender
charity, watch over our country and those who are serving
it. Obtain courage and strength for their loved ones. On
earth your heart overflowed with compassion for those in
danger or distress. In heaven you have never failed those
who called on you with confidence. I know you will not fail
me now; that you will help me always to remain close to
our Lord, who is the divine Protector of mankind.
O powerful wonder-worker, in this hour of
need obtain what I ask of you. Amen.

Prayer to St. Augustine
Feast Day 28th August

ST. AUGUSTINE'S PRAYER TO THE HOLY SPIRIT

Breathe in me, O Holy Spirit,
that my thoughts may all be holy.
Act in me, O Holy Spirit,
that my words may be holy.
Move in me, Holy Spirit,
that my work too may be holy.
Attract my heart, Holy Spirit,
that I may love only what is holy.
Strengthen me, Holy Spirit,
that I may defend all that is holy.
Protect me, Holy Spirit
that I may always be holy.

Prayer to St. Benedict
Feast Day 11th July

Glorious St. Benedict who taught us the way to religious perfection by the practice of self-conquest, mortification, humility, obedience, prayer, silence, retirement and detachment from the world, I kneel at your feet and humbly beg you to take my present need under your special protection (mention here). Vouchsafe to recommend it to the Blessed Virgin Mary and lay it before the throne of Jesus. Cease not to intercede for me until my request is granted. Above all, obtain for me the grace to one day meet God face to face, and with you and Mary and all the angels and saints to praise Him through all eternity. O most powerful Saint Benedict, do not let me lose my soul, but obtain for me the grace of winning my way to heaven, there to worship and enjoy the most holy and adorable Trinity forever and ever. Amen.

Edel Quinn

The venerable Edel Mary Quinn (September 14, 1907 - May 12, 1944) was an Irish Lay Missionary. Born in Kanturk, Co. Cork. Edel felt a call to religious life at a young age. She wished to join the Poor Clares but was prevented by advanced tuberculosis. After spending eighteen months in a sanatorium, her condition unchanged, she decided to become active in the Legion of Mary, which she joined in Dublin at the age of 20. She gave herself completely to its work in the form of helping the poor in the slums of Dublin. In 1936, at age 29 and dying of tuberculosis, Edel became a Legion of Mary Envoy, a very active missionary to East and Central Africa, departing in December 1936 for Mombassa. By the outbreak of World War II she was working as far off as Dar es Salaam and Mauritius. Fighting her illness in seven and a half years she established hundreds of Legion branches and councils in today's Tanzania, Kenya, Uganda, Malawi and Mauritius. Her health was not good, she died in Nairobi, Kenya of tuberculosis in May 1944. She is buried there in the Missionaries' Cemetery. The cause for her beatification was introduced in 1956. She was declared venerable by Pope John Paul II on December 15, 1994.

Eternal Father, I thank You for the grace you gave to your servant, Edel Quinn, of striving to live always in the joy of Your presence, for the radiant charity infused into her heart by Your Holy Spirit, and for the strength she drew from the Bread of Life to labour until death for the glory of Your Name, in loving dependence on Mary, Mother of the Church. Confident, O Merciful Father, that her life was pleasing to You, I beg You to grant me through her intercession the special favour I now implore... and to make known by miracles the glory she enjoys in Heaven, so that she may be glorified also by Your Church on earth, through Christ Our Lord. Amen.

St. Faustina
Feast Day 5th October

St. Faustina was born on 25th August 1905 in Glogoweic, Poland. When she was almost twenty, she entered the Congregation of the Sisters of Our Lady of Mercy, whose members devoted themselves to the care and education of troubled young women. In the 1930's Sister Faustina received a message of mercy from the Lord, that she was told to spread throughout the world. She was asked to become a model of how to be merciful to others, and an instrument for God's plan of mercy for the world. She worked vigorously with Jesus for the salvation of lost souls, even to the extent of offering her life as a sacrifice for sinners. Her life was marked with the stigma of suffering, but also with extraordinary graces. Sister Faustina died from tuberculosis on 5th October 1938 at the age of 33. After her death even her closest associates were surprised as they discovered the great sufferings and mystical experiences Faustina had endured. The message that Sister Faustina received is now being spread throughout the world. Her diary, Divine Mercy in my Soul, has become the handbook for devotion to the Divine Mercy.

"O Jesus, I want to live in the present moment, to live as if this were the last day of my life. I want to use every moment scrupulously for the greater glory of God, to use every circumstance for the benefit of my soul. I want to look upon everything from the point of view that nothing happens without the will of God. God of unfathomable mercy, embrace the whole world and pour Yourself out upon us through the merciful Heart of Jesus". (Diary 1183)

Prayer to Blessed Charles de Foucauld
Feast Day 1st December

Father,
I abandon myself into Your hands.
Do with me what You will.
Whatever You may do,
I thank You.
I am ready for all,
I accept all.

Let only Your Will be done, in me,
and in all Your creatures.
I wish no more than this, O Lord.

Into Your Hands I commend my soul;
I offer it to You, with all the love of my heart,
for I love You, Lord,
and so need to give myself,
to surrender myself into Your hands,
without reserve, and with boundless confidence,
for You are my Father.

Prayer to St. Francis of Assisi
Feast Day 4th October

Lord, make me an instrument of Your peace.
Where there is hatred .... let me sow love.
Where there is injury ... pardon.
Where there is doubt ..... faith.
Where there is despair ... hope.
Where there is darkness .... light.
And where there is sadness.... joy.

O Divine Master, grant that I may not so much seek to be
consoled, as to console; to be understood, as to
understand; to be loved, as to love; for it is in giving that
we receive; it is in pardoning that we are pardoned; and, it
is in dying that we are born to eternal life. Amen.

Dear St. Francis, once worldly and vain, you became
humble and poor for the sake of Jesus and had an
extraordinary love for the Crucified, which showed itself in
your body by the imprints of Christ's Sacred Wounds.
Teach us great love for the poor and loyalty to the
Vicar of Christ. Amen.

Prayer to St. Gerard Majella
Feast Day 16th October
St. Gerard was born at Muro Italy in 1726. After his father died,
when he was a child he was an apprentice to a tailor. In 1749
Gerard entered the Congregation of the Most Holy Redeemer.
(The Redemptorists)

Novena to St. Gerard Majella
O Most Blessed Trinity, I your unworthy creature, thank
you for all the gifts and privileges which you have granted
to St. Gerard, especially for those virtues with which You
have adorned him on earth and the glory which You impart
to him in heaven. Accomplish your work, O Lord, for the
greater glory of the Holy Church. Glorify him before men
and women and through his merits, in union with those of
Jesus and Mary, grant me the grace for which I ask ...
(Mention your intentions)
And you, my powerful intercessor, St. Gerard, always
so ready to help those who have recourse to you. Pray
also for me. Prostrate yourself before the throne of Divine
Mercy and do not leave it without being heard. To you I
confide this important and urgent affair. Graciously take my
cause in hand and let me not end this novena without
having experienced in some way the effects
of your intercession. Amen.

Prayer to St. Joseph
Feast Day 19th March

Oh St. Joseph whose protection is so great, so strong, so
prompt before the Throne of God. I place in you
all my interests and desires.

Oh St. Joseph assist me by your powerful
intercession and obtain for me from your Divine Son all
spiritual blessings through Jesus Christ, Our Lord; so that
having engaged here below your heavenly power I may
offer my thanksgiving and homage to the
most loving of fathers.

Oh St. Joseph, I never weary contemplating you and
Jesus asleep in your arms. I dare not approach while
He reposes near your heart.

Press him in my name and kiss His fine head for me, and
ask Him to return the kiss when I draw my dying breath.
St. Joseph,
patron of departing souls, pray for us. Amen.

Prayer to St. Jude
Feast Day 28th October

Among this historic Twelve the least known was the
Apostle Jude. Today however he is loved and honoured by
many, who call him the saint of the impossible.
In his honour we pray:

Most holy Apostle Saint Jude, faithful servant and friend of
Jesus, the name of the traitor who delivered the beloved

Master into the hands of His enemies has caused you to be forgotten by many, but the Church honours and invokes you universally as the patron of hopeless cases, of things almost despaired of.

Pray for me, I am so helpless and alone. Make use I implore you, of that particular privilege given to you, to bring visible and speedy help, where help is almost despaired of. Come to my assistance in this great need, that I may receive the consolations and help of heaven in all my necessities, tribulations and sufferings, (*here make your request*) and that I may bless God with you and all the elect forever.

I promise, O blessed Saint Jude, to be ever mindful of this great favour, to always honour you as my special and powerful patron, and to gratefully encourage devotion to you. Amen.

Prayer to St. Martin De Porres
Feast Day 3rd November

To you Saint Martin de Porres we prayerfully lift up our hearts filled with serene confidence and devotion. Mindful of your unbounded and helpful charity to all levels of society and also of your meekness and humility of heart, we offer our petitions to you. Pour out upon our families the precious gifts of your solicitous and generous intercession; show to the people of every race and every colour the paths of unity and of justice; implore from our Father in heaven the coming of his kingdom, so that through mutual benevolence in God men may increase the fruits of grace and merit the rewards of eternal life. Amen.

Prayer for the Beatification of
Venerable Matt Talbot, Servant of God

Lord, in your servant, Matt Talbot you have given us a wonderful example of triumph over addiction, of devotion to duty, and of lifelong reverence of the Holy Sacrament. May his life of prayer and penance give us courage to take up our crosses and follow in the footsteps of Our Lord and Saviour, Jesus Christ. Father, if it be your will that your beloved servant should be glorified by your Church, make known by your heavenly favours the power he enjoys in your sight. May Matt Talbot's triumph over addiction bring hope to our community and strength to our hearts.
We ask this through the same Jesus Christ
Our Lord. Amen.

Prayer to St. Michael The Archangel
Feast Day 29th September

Saint Michael the Archangel, defend us in battle be our protection against the wickedness and snares of the devil. May God rebuke him, we humbly pray; and do thou, O prince of the heavenly host, by the power of God, thrust into hell Satan and all evil spirits who wander through the world for the ruin of souls. Amen.

Novena to St. Michael The Archangel

Saint Michael the Archangel, loyal champion of God and His people, I turn to you with confidence and seek your powerful intercession. For the love of God, who made you so glorious in grace and power, and for the love of the Mother of Jesus, the Queen of the Angels, be pleased to hear my prayer. You know the value of my soul in the eyes of God. May no stain of evil ever disfigure its beauty. Help me to conquer the evil spirit who tempts me. I desire to imitate your loyalty to God and Holy Mother Church and your great love for God and people. And since you are God's messenger for the care of His people, I entrust to you this special request: (*Mention your request*).

St. Michael, since you are, by the will of the creator, the powerful intercessor of christians, I have great confidence in your prayers. I earnestly trust that if it is God's holy will my petition will be granted.

Pray for me, St. Michael, and also for those I love. Protect us in all dangers of body and soul. Help us in our daily needs. Through your powerful intercession, may we live a holy life, die a happy death, and reach heaven where we may praise and love God with you forever. Amen.

St. Peter and St. Paul

Feast Day 29th June
St. Augustine writes (Sermon 295):
Both apostles share the same feast day, for these two were one; and even though they suffered on different days, they were as one. Peter went first, and Paul followed. And so we celebrate this day made holy for us by the apostles' blood. Let us embrace what they believed, their life, their labours, their sufferings, their preaching, and their confession of faith.

Prayer to St. Peter and St. Paul

Almighty God, whose blessed apostles Peter and Paul glorified you by their martyrdom, grant that your Church, instructed by their teaching and example, and knit together in unity by your Spirit, may ever stand firm upon the one foundation, which is Jesus Christ our Lord; who lives and reigns with you, in the unity of the Holy Spirit, one God, for ever and ever.

Matthew 16:18

Jesus says. "That thou art Peter, and upon this rock I will build my church".

First Letter of St. Paul to the Corinthians

Let no one seek his own good, but the good of others.

Prayer to St. Peregrine

Feast day 1st May

O God, In St. Peregrine you gave us an outstanding example of faith and patience. We humbly ask you that, by imitating him and by help of his prayers, we may believe more fully in your healing help, bear the suffering of his life without wavering, and come with joy to the peace of heaven. We ask this through Jesus Christ, our Lord. Amen.

Saint Peregrine,
you have given us an example to follow;
as a Christian you were steadfast in love;
as a Servite, you were faithful in service;
as a penitent you humbly acknowledged your sin;

afflicted you bore suffering with patience.
Intercede for us, then,
with our heavenly Father so that
we steadfast, humble and patient may
receive from Jesus Christ the grace we ask.

Prayer to St. Philomena
The Rosary in honour of Saint Philomena

The Rosary also known as the chaplet or Little Crown of Saint Philomena is made up of red beads to signify her martyrdom and white beads; a token of her virginity and purity.

This rosary is one of the simplest ways of praying to the Saint. First the creed is recited on the Crucifix or the medal of St. Philomena to ask the gift of faith. Three Our Fathers on each of the white beads to thank the Blessed Trinity for the gifts given to the Holy Virgin, for in whose honour, she laid down her life. The red beads are thirteen in number and signify the thirteen years our martyr lived on earth and this prayer is recited on each bead:

Hail, O Holy Saint Philomena, my dear patroness. As my advocate with thy Divine Spouse, intercede for me now and at the hour of my death.

Saint Philomena, beloved daughter of Jesus and of Mary, pray for us who have recourse to thee. Amen.

At the end say:

Hail, O Illustrious Saint Philomena, who so courageously shed thy blood for Christ, I bless the Lord for all the graces He has bestowed upon thee, during thy life especially

103

at thy death, I praise and glorify Him for the honour and power with which he has crowned thee, and I beg you to obtain for me from God the graces I ask through thy intercession. Amen

(This prayer may be substituted for thirteen Hail Mary's each followed by: *Saint Philomena, pray for us.*)

Prayer to St. Pio
Feast Day 23rd September

"Pray, pray to the Lord with me, because the whole world needs prayer. And every day, when your heart especially feels the loneliness of life, pray. Pray to the Lord, because even God needs our Prayers."

WORDS OF ST. PIO

Prayer for the Intercession of
St. Pio of Pietrelcina

Dear God, You generously blessed Your servant, St. Pio of Pietrelcina, with the gifts of the Spirit. You marked his body with the five wounds of Christ Crucified, as a powerful witness to the saving Passion and Death of Your Son. Endowed with the gift of discernment, St. Pio laboured endlessly in the confessional for the salvation of souls. With reverence and intense devotion in the celebration of the Mass, he invited countless men and women to a greater union with Jesus Christ in the Sacrament of the Holy Eucharist. Through the intercession of St. Pio of Pietrelcina, I confidently beseech You to grant me the grace of (*here state your petition*). Amen

Glory be to the Father... (three times).

St. Rita

Saint Rita's Miracles involve her devotion to the suffering Christ. Pictures of Saint Rita often show her holding a Crucifix because a thorn fell from a replica of the suffering Christ and had pierced Rita's forehead; the stigma which bled for fifteen years before her death. The wound was said to have festered and gave off a putrid odour which caused her to ask to be confined to a room. The nuns in the Monastery of Mary Magadalene initially objected to her presence on the pretence that her dead husband's enemies might invade the convent. When the patron saints of St. Rita provided her access into the convent, the nuns could not deny her and over the years they grew to love her. In the final years of her life, St. Rita was bedridden. Still, St. Rita, Saint of the Impossible Causes, incurable illness and abusive relationships, taught and prayed, offering aid however she could from her bed in the confines of her room until her death on May 22, 1457.

Prayer to St. Rita
Feast Day 22nd May

O powerful St. Rita, rightly called the Saint of the Impossible, I come to you with confidence in my great need. You know well my trials, for you yourself were many times burdened in this life. Come to my help, speak for me, pray with me, intercede on my behalf before the Father. I know that God has a most generous heart and that he is a most loving Father. Join your prayers to mine and obtain for me the grace I desire (make your request). You who were so very pleasing to God on earth and are so much now in heaven, I promise to use this favour, when granted, to better my life, to proclaim God's mercy, and to make you more widely known and loved. Amen.

Prayer to St. Therese of Lisieux
(Also known as the Little Flower)
Feast Day 1st October

O little St. Therese of the Child Jesus, who during your short life on earth became a mirror of angelic purity, of love strong as death, and of wholehearted abandonment to God, now that you rejoice in the reward of your virtues, cast a glance of pity on me as I leave all things in your hands. Make my troubles your own - speak a word for me to our Lady Immaculate, whose flower of special love you were - to that Queen of heaven "who smiled on you at the dawn of life." Beg her as the Queen of the heart of Jesus to obtain for me by her powerful intercession, the grace I yearn for so ardently at this moment, and that she join with it a blessing that may strengthen me during life. Defend me at the hour of death, and lead me straight on to a happy eternity. Amen.

"My whole strength lies in prayer and sacrifice, these are my invincible arms; they can move hearts far better than words, I know it by experience".

"I have not the courage to force myself to seek beautiful prayers in books; not knowing which to choose I act as children do who cannot read: I say quite simply to the good God what I want to tell Him, and He always understands me".

WORDS OF ST. THERESE

St. Vincent de Paul

Feast Day 27th September

*He established the Congregation of the Mission of Priests
and the Sisters of Charity. The Society of St. Vincent de
Paul, founded in 1833 by Frederic Ozanam, continues
his work to this day. St. Vincent's charity for the poor,
the downtrodden, the young, the elderly, the refugees,
the slaves was astonishing to others. He searched for
abandoned children and organised groups to help those in
need. He built homes for the poor, the sick, the abandoned
children, and provided care for the elderly.*

Prayer to St. Vincent de Paul

St. Vincent, patron of all charitable associations and father
of those in need, come to our assistance. Obtain from Our
Lord help for the poor, relief for the infirm, consolation
for the afflicted, protection for the abandoned, a spirit of
generosity for the rich, and grace of conversion for sinners.
May we be united in the life to come, by your intercession.
Amen.

St. Mary MacKillop
Patroness of Australia
Feast Day 8th August

Mary Helen MacKillop (15th January 1842 - 8th August 1909), also known as Saint Mary of the Cross, was an Australian Roman Catholic nun who, together with Father Julian Tenison Woods founded the Sisters of St. Joseph of the Sacred Heart and a number of schools and welfare institutions throughout Australasia with an emphasis on education for the poor, particularly in country areas. Since her death she has attracted much veneration in Australia and internationally.

On 17th July 2008, Pope Benedict XVI prayed at her tomb during his visit to Sydney for world Youth Day 2008. On 19th December 2009, Pope Benedict XVI approved the Roman Catholic Church's recognition of a second miracle attributed to her intercession. She was canonised on 17th October 2010 during a public ceremony in St. Peter's Square at the Vatican.

Prayer to St. Mary MacKillop
Ever generous God,
You inspired Saint Mary MacKillop
to live her life faithful to the Gospel of Jesus Christ
and constant in bringing hope and encouragement
to those who were disheartened, lonely or needy.
With confidence in your generous providence
and through the intercession of Saint Mary MacKillop
we ask that you grant our request.........
we ask that our faith and hope be fired afresh by
the Holy Spirit

so that we too, like Mary MacKillop, may live with courage,
trust and openness.
Ever generous God hear our prayer.
We ask this through Jesus Christ. Amen.

St. George
Patron Saint of England
Feast Day 23rd April

*St. George is the patron Saint of England. His emblem, a
red cross on a white background, is the flag of England,
and part of the British flag. St George's emblem was
adopted by Richard The Lion Heart and brought to
England in the 12th century. The king's soldiers wore it on
their tunics to avoid confusion in battle.*

*St. George is believed to have been born in Cappadocia
(now Eastern Turkey) in the year A.D. 270. He was a
Christian. At the age of seventeen he joined the Roman
army and soon became renowned for his bravery. He
served under a pagan Emperor but never forgot
his Christian faith.*

*When the pagan Emperor Diocletian started persecuting
Christians, St. George pleaded with the Emperor to spare
their lives. However, St. George's pleas fell on deaf ears
and it is thought that the Emperor Diocletian tried to make
St. George deny his faith in Christ, by torturing him. St
George showed incredible courage and faith and was
finally beheaded near Lydda in Palestine on
23rd April, 303.*

*In 1222, the Council of Oxford declared 23rd April to be
St George's Day*

In 1415, 23rd April was made a national feast day.

Prayer to St. George

O God, who didst grant to Saint George strength and constancy in the various torments which he sustained for our holy faith; we beseech Thee to preserve, through his intercession, our faith from wavering and doubt, so that we may serve Thee with a sincere heart faithfully unto death.
Through Christ our Lord.
Amen.

St. Patrick
Patron Saint of Ireland
Feast Day 17th March

Patrick was born around 385 in Scotland, probably Kilpatrick. His parents were Calpurnius and Conchessa, who were Romans living in Britain in charge of the colonies. As a boy around fourteen years of age he was captured and taken to Ireland as a slave to herd and tend sheep. Ireland at this time was a land of Druids and pagans. He learned the language and practices of the people who held him.

During his captivity, he turned to God in prayer. Patrick's captivity lasted until he was twenty, when he escaped after a dream from God in which he was told to leave Ireland by going to the coast. There he found some sailors who took him back to Britain, where he reunited with his family. He had another dream in which the people of Ireland were calling out to him "We beg you, holy youth, to come and walk among us once more".

He began his studies for the priesthood. He was ordained by St. Germanus, the Bishop of Auxerre, whom he had studied under for years. Later, Patrick, was ordained a bishop, and was sent to take the Gospel to Ireland. Patrick preached the gospel throughout Ireland, converting many. Patrick preached and converted for forty years. He died at Saul, where he had built the first church. Patrick used the shamrock to explain the Trinity.

St. Patrick's Breastplate
Christ with me
Christ before me
Christ behind me
Christ below me
Christ within me
Christ at my right hand
Christ at my left hand
Christ in every
ear that hears me
Christ in every
eye that sees me
Christ in every mouth
that speaks of me
Christ in every heart
that thinks of me

St. Andrew
Patron Saint of Scotland
Feast Day 30th November

In Greek Andrew means 'manly'. He was born between AD 5 and AD 10 in Bethsaida, the principal fishing port of Palestine. His parents were Jona and Joanna; his brother was Simon. Jona, along with his business-partner and friend Zebedee and his sons James and John, was a fisherman.

On the banks of the Jordan, Andrew met John the Baptist: he was the first disciple and the first apostle. It was he who brought the boy with the loaves and fishes to Jesus before the feeding of the five thousand.

According to the apocryphal 'Acts of Andrew' he is said to have travelled to Asia Minor and the Black Sea. In the city of Synope he is believed to have suffered great hardships and the house he was in was nearly burnt down. He returned twice more to Asia Minor and Greece, even travelling as far as Hungary, Russia and to the banks of the Oder in Poland.

In Patras, he was given the choice of being offered as a sacrifice to the gods or being scourged and crucified. By his own request the cross was diagonal. He, like his brother Peter, felt himself unworthy to be crucified on the upright cross of Christ.

He hung for three days on the cross, fixed not by nails but by rope round his hands and feet. Even in his last agony, he continued to preach.

About the middle of the 10th century, Andrew became the patron saint of Scotland. History states that the relics of Andrew were brought under supernatural guidance from Constantinople to the place where the modern town of St. Andrew stands today.

Prayer to St. Andrew

St. Andrew, you were the first to recognise and follow the Lamb of God. With your friend St. John you remained with Jesus for that first day, for your entire life, and now throughout eternity. As you led your brother St. Peter to Christ and many others after him, draw us also to him. May we be like you in sharing friendship and hospitality, and in faithfulness to Jesus and his kingdom of justice, love and peace. May our country be a community in which everyone matters, everyone has an honoured place, and the dignity of each is assured by our faith in you as Father of us all. We ask this through Christ our Lord.
AMEN

St. David
Patron Saint of Wales
Feast Day 1st March
St. David (Welsh : Dewi Sant) was born towards the end of the fifth century. He was a scion of the royal house of Ceredigion, and founded a Celtic monastic community at Glyn Rhosin (The Vale of Roses) on the western headland of Sir Benfro, at the spot where St David's Cathedral stands today. David's fame as a teacher and ascetic spread throughout the Celtic world. His foundation at Glyn Rhosin became an important Christian shrine and the most important centre in Wales. The date of Dewi Sant's death is recorded as 1st March, but the year is uncertain, possibly 588. As his monks prepared for his death St. David uttered these words: 'Brothers be ye constant.

The yoke which with single mind ye have taken, bear ye to the end; and whatsoever ye have seen with me and heard, keep and fulfil'.

To celebrate this day, people wear a symbol of either a leek or daffodil. The leek arises from an occasion when a troop of Welsh were able to distinguish each other from a troop of English enemy dressed in similar fashion by wearing leeks. An alternative emblem developed in recent years is the daffodil.

Prayer to St. David

Almighty God, who called your servant David to be a faithful and wise steward of your mysteries for the people of Wales, mercifully grant that, following his purity of life and zeal for the gospel of Christ, we may with him receive the crown of everlasting life; through Jesus Christ our Lord, who lives and reigns with you and the Holy Spirit, one God, now and ever. Amen.

Calendar of Saints

St. Teilo 9th
St. Scholastica.. 10th
St. Gobnait... 11th
St. Cyril, St. Methodius, St. Valentine.............................. 14th
Seven Servite Founders, St. Fintan................................. 17th
St. Peter Damian 21st
Chair of St. Peter, Apostle 22nd
St. Polycarp 23rd
St. Oswald 28th

March
St. David - Patron Saint of Wales......................................1st
St. Casimir 4th
St. Colette.. 6th
St. Perpetua, St. Felicity 7th
St. John of God, St. Senan... 8th
St. Frances of Rome... 9th
St. John Ogilvie 10th
St. Aengus... 11th
St. Louise... 15th
St. Patrick - Patron Saint of Ireland 17th
St. Cyril of Jerusalem 18th
St. Joseph.. 19th
St. Enda...21st
St. Turibius de Mongrovejo... 23rd

April
St. Francis of Paola 2nd
St. Richard... 3rd
St. Isidore 4th
St. Vincent Ferrer 5th
St. John Baptist de la Salle.. 7th
St. Stanislaus of Krakow... 11th

St. Martin I, Pope.. 13th
St. Bernadette.. 16th
St. Laserian 18th
St. Beuno... 20th
St. Anselm 21st
St. George - Patron Saint of England 23rd
St. Adalbert of Prague 23rd
St. Fidelis of Sigmaringen.. 24th
St. Mark 25th
St. Peter Chanel, St. Louis Grignon de Montford 28th
St. Catherine of Siena 29th
St. Pius V, Pope 30th

May

St. Joseph The Worker...1st
St. Athanasius 2nd
St. Philip and St. James, Apostles..................................... 3rd
The English Martyrs.. 4th
St. Asaph... 5th
St. Comgall 10th
St. Achilleus, St. Nereus, St. Pancras 12th
St. Matthias... 14th
St. Carthage 15th
St. Brendan... 16th
St. Paschal 17th
St. John, I Pope 18th
St. Dunstan... 19th
St. Bernardine of Siena 20th
St. Rita.. 22nd
St. Bede The Venerable, St. Gregory VII Pope............. 25th
St. Mary Magdalen of Pazzi.. 25th
St. Philip Neri.. 26th

August